19.95

Public
Relations
DISASTERS
Talespin

Public Relations Relations DISASTERS

Talespin

inside stories & lessons learnt

GERRY McCUSKER

KOGAN
PAGE

London and Philadelphia

'The man who makes no mistakes does not usually make anything.'

Edward John Phelps, 1822–1900

This book is dedicated to anyone who has ever made a mistake, been brave enough to admit it and who has become a little more human as a result of the experience.

And to Mum, Dad, James and Chris.

Gerry McCusker
geemccee@yahoo.com.au

Publisher's note

Every possible effort has been made to ensure that the information contained in this book is accurate at the time of going to press, and the publishers and authors cannot accept responsibility for any errors or omissions, however caused. No responsibility for loss or damage occasioned to any person acting, or refraining from action, as a result of the material in this publication can be accepted by the editor, the publisher or any of the authors.

First published in Great Britain and the United States in 2005 by Kogan Page Limited as *Talespin*
Paperback edition published in 2006 as *Public Relations Disasters*
Reprinted in 2007

Apart from any fair dealing for the purposes of research or private study, or criticism or review, as permitted under the Copyright, Designs and Patents Act 1988, this publication may only be reproduced, stored or transmitted, in any form or by any means, with the prior permission in writing of the publishers, or in the case of reprographic reproduction in accordance with the terms and licences issued by the CLA. Enquiries concerning reproduction outside these terms should be sent to the publishers at the undermentioned addresses:

120 Pentonville Road	525 South 4th Street, #241
London N1 9JN	Philadelphia PA 19147
United Kingdom	USA
www.kogan-page.co.uk	

© Gerry McCusker, 2005

The right of Gerry McCusker to be identified as the author of this work has been asserted by him in accordance with the Copyright, Designs and Patents Act 1988.

ISBN-10 0 7494 4572 6
ISBN-13 978 0 7494 4572 0

British Library Cataloguing-in-Publication Data

A CIP record for this book is available from the British Library.

Library of Congress Cataloging-in-Publication Data

McCusker, Gerry, 1962-
  [Talespin]
  Public relations disasters : talespin—inside stories and lessons learnt / Gerry McCusker.
    p. cm.
  Previously published in hardback as Talespin (2005).
  ISBN 0-7494-4572-6 (pbk.)
  1. Public relations—Case studies. 2. Public relations—Miscellanea. I. Title.
HM1221.M39 2005
659.2—dc22

                              2006036751

Typeset by Datamatics Technologies Ltd, Mumbai, India
Printed and bound in Great Britain by Thanet Press Ltd, Margate

Contents

Introduction

More loathed than lawyers and more slagged off than salesmen, Public Relations (PR) practitioners are widely regarded as the business types the public trust least. For while doctors are perhaps the most respected of professionals, the spin variety are the least well thought of, with consumer research confirming that PR people are held in even greater contempt than estate agents and advertising gurus. Of course, admissions in the occasional PR industry survey showing that almost one third of consultants admit to having knowingly told fibs about clients to the media, do nothing for PR's own credibility or integrity.

This book details some of the world's most infamous PR disasters, the resultant fallout from them, the lessons that can be learnt and also the absurdity and, the laughs that often accompany the botched PR jobs.

Yet, long before it was perceived to be the most devious of all business disciplines, Public Relations was most succinctly defined as 'the management of reputation'. Nowadays, it's with somewhat perverse irony that PR's own reputation should have such low stock, tarnished as it is by accusations of half-truths, full-blown deceptions and anything in between, which is increasingly referred to as 'spin doctoring'.

This term refers to the practice of presenting information to the media and the public in ways that ensure that the information is both well received and well perceived, regardless of the truth. Consequently, the dubbing of PR consultants as 'spin doctors' has become as derisory and derogatory as the term 'quack' is to medical professionals.

Amazingly, however, PR's worth as the most potent form of business communication has arguably never been stronger. The percentage of marketing budgets allocated to PR is bigger than ever before, the number of undergraduates seeking a career in it is rising rapidly and the number of PR consultants employed worldwide is at an all-time high. Hardly disastrous times!

PR disasters

The phrase 'PR disaster' is most frequently used in newspaper columns and media soundbites where the continual twinning of the terms 'PR' and 'disaster' by journalists and reporters is applied to anything and everything negative that happens to any company or organization.

Many PR practitioners believe that the media's obsessive reporting of the concept of 'spin' has tainted the entire PR discipline. Successive scandals from British politics and American corporate life have given the media regular opportunities to depict PR personnel as constantly embroiled in organizational mishaps. As a result, PR people are portrayed as Machiavellian manipulators of the truth and scheming skewers of public opinion.

So why – with its undeniable and growing influence – has PR become almost synonymous with the word 'disaster'? Perhaps it's because anticipating, averting or managing the fallout from operational mishaps is one of the PR practitioner's principal duties. The job is inherently fraught with potential pitfalls and catastrophes that are predisposed to causing bad news.

Broadly speaking, PR disasters emanate from the following sources:

- Acts of God – natural disasters impact upon various interests and agencies.
- Business operations – company processes or product failures catalyse customer complaints, dissatisfaction and subsequent negative news coverage.
- Corporate moves – organizational changes such as acquisitions or mergers cause discontent or disquiet that becomes worthy of media interest.
- Legalities – contentious issues are debated, then reported upon, in public.

- Rumours – difficult-to-dispel gossip erodes corporate or brand reputation.
- Staff – workplace grievances are mismanaged then erupt, causing negative publicity for the organization concerned.
- Scandal – financial or sexual shenanigans around employees or the workplace become a matter of public interest and comment.

I'd also venture that the PR consultants' pitch to their clients – often guaranteeing them exposure in the media outlet of their choice – makes a stiff rod for their own back. And when you add this to the media's current obsession with 'infotainment' – news with a dollop of 'razzle dazzle' – you have a media agenda which forces PR people to dress up or 'sex-up' information in order to secure media coverage. Contriving to present information that fits the 'infotainment' format, PR practitioners can be led into catastrophic errors of judgement: errors that this book features aplenty.

The PR challenge

Few people really appreciate the difficulty of the PR person's aspirational remit: to create and maintain dialogue between an organization and those people it hopes to influence. In practice, though, most practitioners might settle for influencing without the unnecessary travails of dialogue.

But in media relations for example, just getting a journalist's – far less an audience's – attention calls for a complex mix of creativity, imagination, logistics, execution and monitoring. Then there's the amount of ongoing checking and contingencies that have to be allowed for, to ensure that nothing can possibly go wrong.

But as *Talespin* shows, things have a tendency to go horribly wrong.

Beat up

Talespin is not designed to beat up the PR profession; far from it. Having worked as a PR consultant, communications skills specialist and educator for more than 20 years, I have great respect for and affinity with the craft of PR. Practised properly, it's a job that calls for an all-encompassing range of skills and qualities including creativity, diligence, diplomacy, discretion, ethical behaviour, humility, integrity, leadership, perseverance, restraint, sensitivity, sociability, strategic thinking, vision and a very, very thick hide!

I hope that in relaying how PR can sometimes spin out of control, fellow communicators, journalists and other interested parties can learn the common pitfalls of PR and perhaps how to avoid them. Where relevant, I have tried to offer insight as to how these disasters might have been negated or avoided.

Some of the tales spun in this book are a matter of public record, others the result of recollections made over the phone, a coffee and occasionally a glass or two of red. The latter may explain the lily gilding that surfaces sporadically. Sensitive information may also have been held back from one or two of the tales because the consultant concerned still has links to the company where the disaster was perpetrated. While many of the cases are educational, I'd encourage readers to enjoy the book the way it was written: in good spirit. I personally believe that this is something my fellow PR practitioners should do more often: lighten up and rediscover the tremendous scope for enjoyment in our work.

Special thanks go to those who have helped me in my PR career and in the compilation of this book. Alan Ferguson and Alan McGuinness gave me my first break with Scottish PR firm Proscot, Tim Traverse Healy and the University of Stirling media unit supplied timely inspiration when my faith in the discipline was flagging, and Ptarmigan MD Gordon Forbes signed me to work on some exceptionally enjoyable football accounts. I'm especially grateful to those practitioners who contributed their personal tales and, also, to the journalists who helped uncover some of the cock-ups. The guidance of Pauline Goodwin and my agent Shelley Power, the support from Caron Kanareck plus the subbing skills and friendship of Murray Johnson have all been invaluable.

Talespin suggests that there are two kinds of PR disasters. There are those labelled so by the media, even though they may initially have been circumstantial, legal, managerial, operational or otherwise. Then there are the many previously unreported disasters, where PR personnel were the actual creators of their own private – yet sometimes very public – PR hell.

Ambassadors, Announcements, Astroturfing

Ambassadors – Clearly there's no substitute

Media spin:

'Keane saga exposes high risk of personality ads'

Sunday Business Post

The tactic of using a sports star or celebrity as the public face of a brand has been deployed to great effect on numerous occasions. A 'brand ambassador' can bring a product to life, lending his or her unique personality traits to an otherwise inanimate product. And, when the star is in the media spotlight, the brand is able to use PR tactics to increase its own profile – gaining fame by association – and secure a greater share of media voice.

The Pepsi-owned soft drink brand 7UP sought to 'up' its visibility and credibility by making the Republic of Ireland and Manchester United soccer captain, Roy Keane, its 'ambassador' in the Emerald Isle.

Keane to communicate

The deal with the Hibernian hard man known affectionately as 'Keano', was an absolute beano for 7UP and its biggest-ever promotion in the Republic of Ireland. The soft drink hooked up with Ireland's most famous sporting son at a time when the Irish team was about to compete in the world's biggest and most watched soccer tournament, the World Cup in 2002. The deal allowed 7UP to use Keane's picture in a national advertising promotion that boldly asserted that when it comes to soft drinks, 'Clearly there's no substitute'.

At this time, 7UP was also the sole sponsor of the Irish Schoolboys Football Association, so intended to use Keane to influence kids, its key target audience. The 'Clearly There's No Substitute' slogan resonated strongly given that Keane was viewed as an immovable foundation stone in Ireland's attempt to do well in the Korea/Japan tournament. Keano's immediately recognizable, stone-chiselled face was featured on 7UP billboards, cans, bottles, packaging and in-store merchandise and he also appeared in TV and radio advertisements courtesy of a reputed £750,000 marketing spend.

Sending-off offence

As news of the sponsorship hit news pages everywhere, awareness of 7UP – and its involvement with the apparently indispensable Keane – went sky high, doubtless sending the 7Uppers into seventh heaven.

However, in the team's pre-tournament preparations, the fiery-tempered Keane was involved in a major bust up with the team's manager and former Ireland international, Mick McCarthy. It was widely reported that Keane had launched a vitriolic attack on what he believed were his country's shambolic pre-tournament preparations. In front of a full squad meeting, Keane directed his ire at manager McCarthy calling into question his capability, suitability, nationality and, as ranting sports stars are wont to do, his parentage.

McCarthy, sensing his authority not so much being undermined as blown to smithereens, consulted the squad's senior players and officials. Labelling playmaker Keane as 'a disruptive influence', they sent the hot-headed captain home to Ireland. The spat polarized the entire Irish nation. Most adored Keano, but felt angry that he was letting their team down by his self-engineered exclusion.

Meanwhile 7UP's position was becoming uncomfortable to say the least. All over Ireland, people were defacing 7UP's Roy Keane posters and publicity material. Their anger was directed at the brand that was providing visible and painful reminders of the nation's angst.

7UP couldn't disassociate itself from Keane, the public face – albeit a red one – of the brand. Changing its campaign or ordering a product recall at such a late stage would also have cost the brand a fortune and shown it to be weak-willed. Yet every time Keane commented on the spat – and the media hung on his every word – it cast the 7UP brand in a particularly unflattering light, especially given the player's surly intransigence. The irony of the situation facing 7UP was reaffirmed when the Football Association of Ireland drafted in a virtually unknown player to replace Keane.

Clearly, there *was* a substitute.

Attacking options

The 7UP brand was thrust into crisis management mode and controversy by a petulant display of temper from someone who had been paid a handsome sum to be its ambassador. 7UP had aligned itself with Keane, believing that the player granted it proxy access to the hearts of the Irish nation. Yet this incident makes it easy to see how involvement with celebrities and sports stars is a double-edged sword.

Did no one at 7UP think to question the wisdom of sponsoring a player whose abrasiveness, volatility, conceit and 'play hard' lifestyle were widely known? To borrow or hire Keane's good character traits – passionately Irish, unflinchingly reliable and a peak performer – necessitated an evaluation of some of his negative ones, too. These included petulance, loner status, lack of respect for others and perhaps emotional immaturity. As many of the ads that Keane had been involved in for a clutch of other sponsors played on his aggressive image, could 7UP really have expected sweetness and light?

LESSONS LEARNT

A brand is a living entity whose image is mirrored by those who are seen as its representatives. Caution and care are required when choosing a brand ambassador, especially one whose self-control and destructive tendencies have a habit of exploding – on and off-the field – with documented regularity.

Announcements – The information superhighway

Prior to the opening of the newly improved South Eastern Freeway in Melbourne, the old road had been dubbed the South Eastern Car Park due to the traffic bottlenecks that regularly built up, particularly around peak traffic hours.

Motorists demanded improvements to the roads infrastructure and, faced with mounting pressure, the South Eastern Freeway project became a top priority for the local transport authority, VicRoads.

Following an extensive series of major project works, the new freeway was completed with VicRoads' management looking to bask in the glory of their splendid work by making a very public announcement of the road's opening. In fact, the project was such a success that the authority's management decided to handle the media relations effort themselves, dispensing with the need for input from its in-house communications team.

A central reservation

Against the strongest of advice from the authority's in-house PR staff, who clearly saw a PR pile-up in the making, the management team arranged an onsite media photocall for 4 pm in the afternoon. The PR team's concerns were waved aside. Apparently, 4 pm was the only time that all the VIPs from the roads authority could agree on a window in their diaries. One insider later suggested that the time was actually chosen to coincide with the home journey of one fairly important – or self-important – bureaucrat.

To create the impression of clear and uncongested roads for media purposes, several lanes were closed off so the management team could cut a ribbon at an opening ceremony. This caused a traffic snarl-up that far outstripped anything the old South Eastern Car Park had ever been able to generate. Motorists and media alike were quickly up in arms about the lunacy of the self-congratulatory indulgences of the officials involved in declaring the route open.

Hazard warning

Talk radio was the first to vent, damning the bungling bureaucrats and totally overlooking the fact that they had successfully completed an impressive piece of civil engineering infrastructure. The radio coverage raged, further fuelled by the well-intentioned but hapless intervention of the wife of one of the project's engineers. She called the lead talk radio station to offer a spirited defence of her husband and his colleagues who, she insisted, had worked tirelessly on the project. Her unscripted intervention only served to prolong the on-air debate, elevating its significance on the media radar. This encouraged the evening TV news and several scribes to add their take on the bungled announcement. Everyone certainly knew about the new freeway after that!

LESSONS LEARNT

Clearly, this episode shows the folly of allowing egos to dominate where common sense should prevail. Quite simply, the lure of self-aggrandizement should never supersede the needs of the audience you wish to communicate with. So, what could the PR person have done to preclude this event, especially when the whole shebang was instigated and personally championed by the organization's top executives?

Ideally, PR should be represented on every executive management team so the PR implications of any decision can be evaluated and planned for. But if not, the PR person can do nothing but simply wait for the furore to die down and look for opportunities to repair the damage to the organization's battered and maligned reputation. In this case, it looked like a long road back.

Astroturfing – PR creates smokescreen

Media spin:

'Behind fuming bar owners is savvy, well-heeled group'

Los Angeles Times

In the early 1990s, when the commercial interests of the big tobacco companies in the United States were coming under increasing pressure from the trend towards 'smoke free' zones in public places, a group sprung up to defend smokers' rights. This is perhaps not surprising in what purports to be the pluralistic home of free speech.

But while the National Smoker's Alliance (NSA) appeared to be an independent body representing the rights of individuals who wanted to smoke, it was eventually revealed to be a sham organization funded by big business and administered by one of the world's largest PR companies.

Paid a packet

Dubbed an 'Astroturf' group due to its fake or synthetic grassroots nature, the NSA was thought to be the brainchild of PR firm Burson Marsteller, who set it up with the backing of several notable 'ciggy biggies' including Philip Morris, Lorillard and Brown & Williamson.

So how do we know it was a fake? Well, we paid heed to the words of Morton Downey, Jr, a former NSA Advisory Board Member who admitted the group was a front for the tobacco industry. That was a big clue. Then there was its funding. Internal Revenue Service documents showed that in its first three years of operation, less than 1 per cent of NSA earnings came from membership dues, which left lots of room for corporate donations.

Although claiming to have a membership of around 3 million people, analysis of the NSA's annual reports by media vigilantes PR Watch revealed that income from membership dues stood at just $74,000 – enough for just 7,400 members. There's a discrepancy – if not a lie – between 3 million and 7,400. In fact, so lacklustre was the response to the NSA's initial membership drive that it eventually ran full-page ads and not only waived joining fees but even paid people to join the group.

While the NSA appeared to be a group that represented the rights of smokers, it was a front for the interests of people who make money from people addicted to nicotine. Its rationale was simple; the fewer places people are allowed to smoke, the less people will smoke and the more this will hurt 'big tobacco's' financial interests.

Ciggy stardust

So what did the NSA do to create its smokescreen? It recruited local businesses – bars, restaurants, etc – whose wallets could be hit by anti-smoking legislation. The NSA showed these businesses how trade and profitability would be adversely affected by legislation that sought to restrict or prohibit smoking. It also showed how the bans infringed upon smokers' rights, of course.

Then, the NSA used these credible businesses as channels for distributing pre-printed master campaign materials – generally created by Burson Marsteller – tailored to contest smoking bans and aimed at local media. The PR puppeteers even seconded their own PR staff to roles as NSA Action Team Leaders, whose job was to run local campaigns. The Leaders' responsibilities included identifying and managing all local media relations and lobbying opportunities and rallying NSA representation at local stakeholder meetings. Nothing was left to chance or, more tellingly, left to any genuine grassroots locals.

No doubts

Clearly, the NSA was not an independent 'smokers' rights' group. It was heavily influenced and bankrolled by the interests of fee-paying clients – tobacco companies – with a vested interest in contesting smoking bans. Until rumbled, the strategy was highly effective at generating media coverage biased towards the pro-smoking lobby and duping a range of news-hungry media. However, the real PR disaster in this case only really surfaced when the PR initiator's cover was blown, uncovering the sleight of hand. The entire PR industry's image also suffered because the NSA and Burson Marsteller had managed to hoodwink media and public audiences and influence legislation before being 'outed'.

This case shows how half-truths provided a smokescreen for tactics deployed in a strategy designed to influence public opinion and further the needs of paying clients. It's no wonder that so many people are suspicious of PR campaigns and the practitioners who carry them out, especially when one of the world's biggest and, it's claimed, most reputable PR firms is involved in initiating and executing a covert campaign such as this.

LESSONS LEARNT

Transparency is one of the fundamental tenets of most of the world's professional PR associations. Member consultancies – including the famous ones – are supposed to conduct their business in an open and honest way, although there are no enforceable rules that seriously penalize or disbar companies who contravene what are, in the final analysis, voluntary guidelines.

This case is also expertly documented by John Stauber and Sheldon Rampton of media vigilante organization, PR Watch, www. prwatch.org.

B

Brands,
Briefings,
Broadcast Media

Brands – Cola brands fizzing after allegations

Media spin:
'India loses faith in Pepsi, Coca-Cola'
Hindustan Times.com

Allegations that two of the world's biggest and best-known brands, Pepsi and Coca-Cola, sold colas in India containing excessive levels of toxic chemicals, were met with unnecessarily belligerent communications responses. India's Centre for Science and Environment (CSE) suggested that the toxin levels far exceeded those permitted in soft drink formulations sold in EU countries, signalling that there was a real PR disaster in the making.

Flat denials

The companies started to fizz when the CSE – a national environmental watchdog – claimed cola samples it had tested contained four toxic chemicals: lindane, DDT, malathion and chlorpyrifos. However, both Pepsi and Coke chose not to respond with concerned or conciliatory tones or even to calmly and confidently call for independent third-party tests to be organized. If they'd done so, they might have exhibited the traits of very human and very professional, socially responsible corporations. Instead, they arrogantly insisted that their products had passed stringent quality tests set by accredited Indian and international laboratories. And their tone of voice in doing so patently upset a lot of people.

Even as Pepsi was insisting that its products were perfectly safe, a government laboratory was confirming that some of its soft drinks had much higher levels of pesticides than EU norms. Pepsi sought to hide behind the supposed endorsement of the Union Health Minister Sushma Swaraj who, Pepsi claimed, had endorsed its product's safety. Presuming that this pronouncement would quell any customer disquiet, Pepsico added with some finality, 'We have nothing further to add.'

It was unfortunate for them, though, that Swaraj did have more to add. Swaraj went on record to re-affirm the findings of much higher pesticide levels than normal, claiming that lindane was present in all the soft drinks tested yet higher by 1.1 to 1.4 times the European norms in 33 per cent of the samples. Talk about lies, damned lies and statistics!

Pep talk

Strong consumer reactions followed these revelations, with the Indian parliament banning its cafeterias from serving Pepsi and Coke. Then, the country's defence ministry also issued a call to its clubs to stop selling the drinks.

As both of the cola rivals continued to strenuously deny that their products exceeded safe limits for pesticide presence, Pepsi publicly challenged the CSE's credibility and, by inference, its findings, and proceeded to legally contest bans issued against its products.

Despite both cola giants welcoming news that the Indian health ministry had agreed to order independent tests, Pepsi talked tough and aggressively filed a writ in Delhi that sought, as one of its goals, High Court intervention against the government itself. Pepsi wanted to prevent the government from acting on the information contained in the CSE report damningly entitled, 'Analysis of Pesticide Residue in Soft Drinks'. Pepsi also sought a restraining order to prevent the CSE from publishing any 'unsubstantiated statements' and to 'withdraw all such material from circulation and its website'.

Any switched-on modern organization knows that any information that has been posted on the Web will circulate and can be retrieved whether or not it stays at the source of its original posting. Like trying to trap air in a butterfly net, Pepsi's legal moves against the CSE were pure folly and only portrayed them as wanting to cover up information relating to its product.

Of course, Pepsi's manoeuvrings merely pepped-up media interest in the story.

Coke edict

Not to be outdone for high-handedness, Coca-Cola filed a case in the Bombay High Court to challenge the Maharashtra government's confiscation of packaged Coke product from a local factory, following the report of the alleged pesticide content. Coke also claimed that the officer who seized the stock did not have the power to do so or to order a ban on the sale and distribution of the seized stock.

Again, this was hardly likely to solicit a favourable response or portray Coke in a positive light as reportage of the case was published. Coke's action breached one of the fundamentals of issues management, which is to try to isolate – and keep attention focused on – the core issue. Challenging an ordinary person's job description or authority did little to quell disquiet or win friends. In fact, Coke's actions could have been construed as the big boys trying to push a little guy around – and the media just love to protect the little guy. Subsequently, the state government countered Coke's position and actually endorsed the ban, saying such powers were permitted by the rules of India's Prevention of Food Adulteration Act.

Things go better with...

Then, things didn't go better with Coke or Pepsi after leaflets (supposedly emanating from Kolkata Municipal Corporation) claimed that both products were safe for consumption. This provoked the wrath of the region's mayor who threatened to take the companies to court, saying that no such certificates had been issued. Again, more fuel for the media fire, and fuel from an authority figure who was officially pronouncing his doubts about both product's safety.

Although one of his underlings did confirm that Kolkata health department officials had indeed conducted the necessary tests and subsequently issued 'reports', the lackey admitted that the tests undertaken did not check for the presence of pesticide residues. By then, the whole affair was surrounded by the unmistakable whiff of underhand dealings and perhaps the suspicion of corruption. Confusion reigned where clarity ought to have shone through.

PR solutions

From a communications perspective, for such strong international brands to behave in such an immature way was quite unbelievable. So many of the watchwords of crisis management went unheeded during what were serious allegations pertaining to public health. Whatever happened to openness, cooperation and proactive resolution, for example?

Although the Indian government eventually vindicated both cola companies, it was no thanks to a puzzling communications response that seems to have been prepared without any consideration of the PR ramifications. The companies may have been prepared to lose a few friends or consumers along the way, but there was really no need to do so. Both brands lost face and left a bitter aftertaste through their cavalier attitude in the face of threats to consumer safety and public health.

LESSONS LEARNT

It's important for companies to be strong, authoritative and above recrimination during crises, but there's little room for aggression or attempts at bullying; someone will eventually take issue with, and maybe even make an issue out of, it. And at the top of the pile of 'must never dos' in the case of emergencies like this, was the decision to pursue litigation. Going to court to suppress information already in the public domain or to contest a marginal issue (such as an official's right to seize stock after it has been well and truly seized!) only elevates the issue's profile and adds new dynamics that the media may think worthy of debate.

Empathy, approachability and responsiveness should have been the prerequisites for handling an issue that could have impacted on the Indian nation's health. Effective PR issues management should have played down the emotionally charged aspects of the case, taking the heat out of the incident, not inflaming it.

Briefings – Master plan Leeds to nowhere

Located in England's industrial North East, Leeds has always had a reputation as a gritty and hardworking town. Its infrastructure, people and general aesthetic reflect that renown. But as the old industrial order petered out, the city needed to look to new ways of regeneration and at a different vision for an all-new future.

When an important development site became available in the heart of the city, a consortium made up of British and Dutch investment partners put together an architectural master plan for the inner city space. The team had the resources and the creative team – led by famed British civic architect Terry Farrell – to put together a winning bid for the site.

Developing support

Part of the strategy to woo the decision-making panel involved trying to put pressure on the council by getting the citizens of Leeds to share the developer's commercial vision of the future. Word of the ambitious plans would be conveyed to the citizens via a media briefing for television, radio and print journalists.

The team's solution was packaged into an elaborate presentation that included architectural plans and schematics plus, as its cornerstone, a scale model of the proposed site accurate down to the tiniest detail.

No expense was spared in assembling the presentation, with the model alone costing close to £30,000.

A media relations specialist was engaged to trumpet news of what the partners saw as their irresistible plan. A city centre photocall was arranged which, on the day, saw a full complement of media in attendance. Introductions to the architectural team and the major fund provider would be made by the PR/MC and the elaborate scale model would be unveiled to a, hopefully, ecstatic reception.

Demolition man

As the consultant stood up to make his master of ceremony introductions flanked by the architect and a representative of the major investor, the doors to the venue opened noisily and one of the developer's senior managers made a beeline for the stage. The consultant interrupted his rehearsed address to ad lib a welcome to the CEO who had obviously made space in his diary to attend the event. The assembled crowd clapped politely.

As the CEO approached the head table, the PR-cum-MC covered the mike with his hand and just as well; the CEO bitterly mumbled curses that indicated that his company had been trumped at the eleventh hour. The circumstances had been scribbled down on a note that he thrust into his PR man's hand. The note revealed that the site had been awarded to a public sector organization for purposes of a more socially altruistic and beneficial nature: a healthcare facility.

Unforeseen development

Obviously upset, the CEO turned on his heels and immediately left the building, leaving his hitherto high-powered delegation to fend for itself. The PR consultant cleared his throat and announced with admirable calm that news of a late development had just come to hand – well, they could all see that it had – and that he required a few seconds to consult with his colleagues.

The guts of the press conference – the reason the media were there – had just evaporated; it was a PR person's nightmare. But help was at hand as both the architect and developer's representative stayed to offer the media their views on the way forward for the city's regeneration, albeit without their cloth-covered development. Showing great magnanimity, the gentlemen and ladies of the press allowed them to say their piece.

In their broadcasts and editorials however, they mercilessly panned the PR gaffe, which was entirely outside the control of the would-be developers or their PR adviser. To this day, it remains one of the briefest PR briefings the consultant concerned has ever been involved in.

LESSONS LEARNT

Influencing key stakeholders can be valuable in trying to corral public opinion, yet identifying which stakeholders are active, passive and latent can help crystallize communications thinking. In this instance, the active stakeholders – the real decision-makers – were in the city council and the non-active audience included the media and the public. It's a very creative–though decidedly tricky–business to use passive and latent stakeholders to influence active stakeholders especially when that old enemy – timing – is lurking in the background. Perhaps resources and energies could have been better spent developing meaningful dialogue with the key decision-makers, whose autonomous decision eventually usurped the best-laid architectural plans.

Broadcast media – PR man of letters

Media spin:
'Bogus letter campaign'

Herald Sun

When Australian radio station owner Austereo saw its chart-topping industry position under threat from foreign-owned competition, it turned to PR gurus Turnbull Porter Novelli (TPN) for communications counsel. Little did Austereo know that the move would see the PR consultants forced to pay compensation to Austereo's competitors, while they themselves would have to issue a humble apology for the tactics pursued by their PR advisers.

Special request

Essentially, one of Turnbull Porter Novelli's then directors, Ken Davis, eventually admitted instigating and executing a bogus, two-year-long, letter-writing campaign intended to discredit a new radio station – Nova FM – which was owned by one of Austereo's competitors, DMG. The smear campaign saw around 50 hoax letters, all signed by a 'Peter Johnston', an imaginary person with a false Melbourne address, who was vociferously opposed to the new radio station.

Letters were also sent to newspapers, community radio stations plus regulators and parliamentarians.

The mystery man's missives were published in the letters pages of several Australian titles including Melbourne broadsheet, *The Age,* and eventually led to a parliamentary radio industry inquiry.

A new spin

Although the inquiry concluded that TPN was ignorant of Davis's actions, Austereo admitted that the letters were aimed at advancing its interests. Saying that he'd composed the letters for personal – not client – reasons, Davis left TPN soon after the revelations came to light. The case proved to be a huge embarrassment both to the consultancy and its client after judges agreed that there was clear evidence of a conspiracy against DMG.

Looking out for number one

For many practitioners working in consultancy, this case also raises the interesting point of accountability. The relationship between the consultancy and the client is usually based on a reporting process that documents and justifies what the consultant is doing in exchange for fees paid. Basically, every client expects to see physical evidence of consultancy activity. Likewise, every consultancy likes to prove to the client exactly how much it is doing to service its needs, support its objectives and, of course, justify its own fees. In this way, the reporting process operates as a kind of ledger detailing adherence to a mutually agreed strategy.

It seems peculiar that throughout the campaign, the 'support' of the fictitious Peter Johnston was never documented or discussed between the agency and client.

It's an unusually trusting client that would give its consultants 'carte blanche' to engage in activity that required neither documentation nor sanction. Similarly, it would be a uniquely generous consultancy that would provide unsung strategic support given that its livelihood hinges on being able to charge fees in exchange for effort expended.

LESSONS LEARNT

In contemporary client/agency relationships, everything must be accounted for, not least the integrity and ethics of all those involved in communicating messages designed to influence stakeholders. As PR people largely deal in the currencies of trust and credibility, any time a practitioner uses deception or trickery to further client interests, the standing of the entire profession, not just the perpetrator, is jeopardized.

Celebrities, Community Relations, Contingency Planning, Crisis Management

Celebrities

The smell of success

After signing up to be the new face of Brut Aftershave, the gifted but eternally wayward English soccer star Paul 'Gazza' Gascoigne announced that it brought him out in a rash and reportedly suggested that aftershave was for 'nancies'.

Low point for brewer

Having agreed to endorse Dansk low alcohol lager, English cricket legend Ian 'Beefy' Botham indiscreetly proclaimed that he wouldn't actually be drinking the 'gnat's piss' himself.

Cosmetic company loses face

Signed up as the new face of Yardley Cosmetics, actress Helena Bonham Carter, unthinkingly forgetting the responsibilities of her new role, told a magazine journalist that she didn't wear make-up.

Community relations – Good intentions turned around

In the spirit of good corporate citizenship, a prominent industrial company decided to sponsor the beautification of a major – and quite overgrown – roundabout located virtually at the gates of its European headquarters. This gesture of goodwill was motivated by the desire to be seen as a responsible corporate partner in a locale where the company was a significant employer, and also out of the need to ensure that an appropriate impression was conveyed to important corporate visitors.

With approval from top management, the firm's communications division liaised with a delighted local council for its blessing to beautify, then briefed a contractor to carry out the work. The communications manager gave express instructions to minimize any impact on traffic flow on what was a busy link to several arterial roads.

Sub-species

Without telling the client, the contractor – with a congested workload of its own – sub-contracted the work to another company where the brief to negate disruption lost something in the translation. The first the company's PR manager knew of this was when his usual morning drive to work was prolonged; traffic was crawling along and he was going to be nearly 45 minutes late for work.

When his mobile rang, it was an irate member of the firm's senior management team similarly trapped in thick traffic. He had just received a call directly from a local radio station asking him why they'd let the beautification of the roundabout start at 8 am, causing tailbacks in all directions.

Unwanted erection

Moreover, there had been a snag in unloading the equipment. The only thing that had been successfully docked and erected was a self-congratulatory sign proclaiming the firm's sponsorship of the works.

These delays had been featured extensively on morning radio traffic reports, mentioning the company headquarters by name and speculating on its likely involvement. The company's switchboard operator's ears were already stinging from stern abuse from motorists trapped in their cars outside the company HQ. The PR man vowed to intercede, but before he could reach his press contacts on his mobile phone, it rang again; it was the local "daily" taking the company to task over the wisdom of starting work at a time when the roundabout was busiest. Suave and empathetic media interview skills plus good working relationships with local scribes prevented an immediate PR wipeout.

Eventually arriving at work, the PR man had to endure the ignominy of having to publicly liaise with the sub-contracting team – who couldn't see what all the fuss was about – as well as the police who had been called to intervene after the impact on traffic. The oaths hurled from passing cars were unflattering to say the least.

The ensuing complaints received by phone and post kept the communications manager and his internal team busy for weeks, with his immediate priority being, somewhat ironically, to rebuild goodwill at a local level.

LESSONS LEARNT

The importance of a written brief, communications oriented or otherwise, and checking that it has been received and understood,
should never be underestimated. Not only does a brief supply clear
instructions as to what action is expected, but it also serves as a
rump-coverer in the event of a crisis. The responsibility of the PR
consultant doesn't just stop at producing communications materials; it extends to managing how the company is perceived in all
facets of its operations. An attentive consultant should be prepared
to move heaven – and earthworks – to see that the company image
is protected.

Contingency planning – In a froth over debt collection

Media spin:
'Nestlé foolish to commit massive PR gaffe'
The Guardian

Sometimes also known as 'scenario planning', contingency planning is the strand of Public Relations devoted to assessing and managing impacts that might be looming on any organization's horizon. Theoretically, Public Relations provides advice to ensure any actions taken by an organization do not adversely affect its repute or standing.

But in 2002, when the coffee and confectionery corporation Nestlé demanded that Ethiopia – the world's poorest state – pay back a debt of £3.7 million while the country was being gripped by its worst famine in 20 years, there was little evidence of any PR forethought or, according to media opinion, any heart.

A lack of rain for the third year in a row had caused the Ethiopian famine and the country's trading clout was coincidentally weakened by a collapse in the price of coffee. In Ethiopia, much of the population gets its livelihood from coffee. In a bitterly ironic twist, Nestlé, the world's largest coffee processor, had recently posted profits in excess of £5 billion.

Bean counters

Nestlé's accountants may have felt totally justified in attempting to reclaim the money – the debt was 25 years overdue – but this cut little ice with those who insisted that the figure demanded would feed a million people in the famine-ravaged country for a month. Subsequently, spokespeople from several international aid agencies voiced their disbelief at Nestlé's actions to the media, saying that Nestlé didn't need the millions. While this emotional claim may have had a ring of truth, it overlooked the fact that as a publicly listed company Nestlé also had responsibilities to its own shareholders and investors. Despite facing exceedingly difficult times, the Ethiopian government offered to pay back immediately what it could afford of the debt to settle the claim, coincidentally offering Nestlé the chance to get a bit of positive PR by appearing as the good guys.

But less than half the money back didn't appease Nestlé as it held fast to its original claim, restating what it saw as the validity of pursuing not so much an aged, but a vintage, commercial debt. The media coverage slated Nestlé for the bad timing of its debt recovery efforts. After all, there's never a good time to chase the world's poorest state for money.

Regular order

This was not the first time that Nestlé had been involved in a pickle over its international dealings. Previously, the corporation was widely criticized for its hard-nosed marketing of baby milk in many of the world's poorest countries. As a result, several eminent figures from the literary world – Germaine Greer, Jeremy Hardy and Will Self – had boycotted an English literary festival partly sponsored by Nestlé. This literary boycott had also generated a lot of negative PR for Nestlé in the mainstream news media. To many, Nestlé was just another large, ruthless and unsympathetic money-making corporation.

So why didn't the company look to the situation with famine-stricken Ethiopia as an opportunity to repair its long-tarnished reputation?

Storm in a teacup

Perhaps it was because Nestlé made a judgement call on what the media were quick to call a PR disaster and how its customers would react to, if even notice, the flak Nestlé was facing. Perhaps the firm thought that it didn't need to court widespread public approval over a justifiable matter of business finances. Plus, when you look at the background to the situation, you see that Nestlé could feel that it was in the right. From its viewpoint, it had bought a German company that owned a majority share in an Ethiopian company. When that firm was seized by the Ethiopian government in the 1970s – without Nestlé's sanction – it was sold to a local firm presumably with some government officials making a tidy profit from the 'acquisition'.

It's possible that Nestlé had quietly imagined that the coverage given to a troublesome trading relationship would not adversely influence consumers in wealthier countries who were already loyal to many popular Nestlé brands. This was a huge miscalculation, however. Nestlé was eventually forced into an embarrassing U-turn after a petition with 40,000 names and consistent exposure of the issue by several influential newspapers, including Britain's *The Guardian*, showed the distaste that the Nestlé stance was creating. Nestlé eventually accepted the original Ethiopian gesture of reparation, also paying the cost of months of bad publicity, too.

LESSONS LEARNT

The reason that this issue was so thorny really lies in the timing of Nestlé pursuit of the debt from Ethiopia. Often, the timing of an organization's actions can be just as critical as its end objective. Ethiopia was in a dire situation, literally unable to offer a better solution than it proposed. Nestlé could easily have shown more empathy, taken the token money offered and the good publicity that would have come with it. The decision over when to cut your losses isn't solely a financial one, as the notion of the triple bottom line – profits, people and the planet – is a contemporary business reality.

Crisis management – Motorists let down by tyre fiasco

Media spin:

'It could be from the textbook of worst PR disasters'

PR Week

When Ford Motor Company's top-selling sport utility vehicle, The Explorer 4×4, drew unwelcome attention as a result of claims that it had an alarming tendency to roll over while being driven, Ford failed to win many friends with its PR response.

The flak included allegations that Bridgestone/Firestone tyres – a standard fit on the Explorer – were principally to blame for adversely affecting the vehicle's safety record. It was claimed that inferior tyre tread caused the vehicles to flip if turned sharply. The gravity of the situation lay in the fact that several incidents were claimed to have resulted in driver deaths.

With mounting concerns and indications of culpability, Ford and Firestone initially tried to stonewall their way through the crisis, insisting that there was no problem. With gall (especially given the linked fatalities), Ford claimed that the accidents could be attributed to incorrect tyre pressure and questionable driving skills. Their lack of concern certainly got customers' and the media's dander up.

Responding to pressure

After revelations over the Explorer came to light and Ford procrastinated rather than taking affirmative action, further exploration of the vehicles by several independent motoring bodies intimated that there was evidence of physical defects in both the Ford and Firestone products. Rather disloyally, Firestone voiced its own concerns that there were product defects in Ford's Explorer that may have contributed to some of the accidents.

But why was no notice paid to the only real option for handing such a serious issue, namely, telling the truth? By following best practice crisis management models, Ford and Firestone should have addressed the safety scare by having top management step forward with honest and frank disclosures. Thereafter, it should have shown its commitment to doing the right thing in the circumstances: making amends for the problems, whatever that entailed.

Ford did step up to the plate, but in a very stylized way: it opted to shoot a slick TV commercial with then company bigwig Jac Nasser glossing over and refuting any problems. But in today's media-savvy world, who really believes what adverts tell you? Maybe someone at Ford felt that a strong rebuttal was required to put the affair to bed. But best practice crisis management models dealing with cases where lives are on the line suggest that humility not hubris is the standard fit.

Hot air

Ford and Firestone's failure to 'front up' and 'fess up' left many questions in the minds of consumers particularly in light of the subsequent investigations into the vehicles. Is the Explorer inherently flawed? Are the Firestone tyres prone to excessive wear? Were the vehicle and the tyres simply a poor match for one another? These were questions that the public was left to speculate on in the information vacuum following the allegations.

Tread carefully

Subsequently, evidence that Ford and Firestone had received reports of tread problems on certain Explorers exported to the Middle East three years before the American crisis occurred, came to light. There were even whispers that company executives were fully aware of the problems and opted not to take action, possibly because of the cost implications of a recall.

What has since been identified as tread separation on the Firestones is thought to have caused around 100 related deaths in the United States and around 47 other fatalities elsewhere in the world. The scandal eventually catalysed the biggest tyre recall in the history of motoring, a move that cost Ford and Firestone dear in dollars and in damage to their respective reputations.

LESSONS LEARNT

Even companies with longstanding heritage need to realize that their reputations are on the line each and every day. Similarly, perceptions of a company can hinge on the incident-to-incident experiences of customers. That's why Ford's initial response to realistic motorist concerns – obfuscation, placation and even denial – did not bring a concerned public onside. Bridgestone's Japanese management also refused to accept any responsibility, impassively blanking calls for investigation, though cultural pressures may have made it difficult for these executives to face the shame and loss of face brought about by perceived 'wrongdoing'. But when operating an international business, it is essential to behave in line with international expectations. Often, however, public liability fears and pressure from legal advisers or insurers will compromise the messages or actions that PR personnel would like to take.

Crises can actually present organizations with the chance to get closer to stakeholder groups. In this case, if concern had been shown over the issue of public safety, Ford and Firestone might have actually garnered greater customer empathy instead of bad press, distrust and temporary lack of faith in their products.

Damage Limitation, Diplomacy, Direct Mail, Disclosure

Damage limitation – Destabilizing the PR effort

Media spin:
'Caught in a moose trap'

The European

Mercedes' launch of its A-Class 'Baby Benz' in late 1997 – a vehicle hailed as the most revolutionary small car since the Mini – veered disastrously off course courtesy of a group of Swedish motoring journalists. The Scandinavian scribes' proprietary vehicle handling test involved trying to swerve the car around an object while driving at high speed, to determine the responsiveness of the vehicle's steering system.

Moose talk

It seems that in Sweden, moose are the objects that most frequently require steering around. Consequently, one journo's attempts to negotiate an imaginary moose at high speed on a press preview day resulted in the scribbling Swede's rolling of the baby Merc. This put a cloud over the car's stability and safety. As the roll had happened at an official media event, the coverage was disastrous. Many other motoring journalists the world over tried to replicate the roll or devise their own version of the moose test. Networked reporting of the incident appeared in media everywhere, putting a noticeable – but ultimately repairable – dent in Mercedes' reputation for design, build quality and safety.

Assembly lines were halted as a major redesign was effected and the public launch of a vehicle that had been exhaustively test-driven for 5 million kilometres was delayed until $300 millions-worth of additional modifications were proven failsafe.

The incident has since passed into motoring folklore as 'The Moose Test' and, the PR disaster notwithstanding, the vehicle looks to have got back on track, on the world's motoring map.

LESSONS LEARNT

Media exposure is often the end game in PR practice. In particular, great effort is made to ensure journalistic attendance at 'media days' where a cohort of targeted media contacts are invited to personally sample and evaluate new products, for example.

In this, however, the 'double-edged sword' analogy becomes especially relevant. Inviting the media to such an event can be akin to throwing a teenage party: you hope everyone will simply have a great and memorable time, yet secretly fear that things might get out of hand.

As the Mercedes A-Class case illustrates, even spending millions in preparation for the event is no guarantee that you can preclude the completely unexpected.

Diplomacy – Love thy neighbour

Media spin:

'Berlusconi Nazi jibe row deepens'

www.cnn.com

Historically, Public Relations has very strong links to international diplomacy, with PR's skills for developing and maintaining cordial relationships between countries much valued over the years. Yet even the impressive theatre that is international politics is not exempt from PR gaffes as was shown in the recent spat between European neighbours Germany and Italy.

A nasty, Nazi jibe

Italy's somewhat abrasive Prime Minister, Silvio Berlusconi, illustrated the simmering enmity between the two countries and nearly set off an international incident when he likened a German Euro MP to a concentration camp commandant. Clearly the remark, echoing Germany's embarrassing Nazi past, was not intended to be complimentary. Berlusconi tried to pass it off as a little joke, but the international community didn't get it and didn't laugh.

Then, possibly taking a cue from his own PM and adding another insult to the injury caused by the first jibe, Italy's Deputy Tourism

Minister Stefano Stefani described German tourists as a horde of arrogant blondes. Completely in step with his PM, Stefano castigated the 'stereotyped blondes', their 'hyper-nationalist pride' as well as their alleged win-at-all-cost mentality.

For good, or bad, measure, Stefano also asserted that the Germans 'noisily invade' Italy's beaches and then chastized a German publication, *Der Spiegel,* for one of its recent magazine covers. It had featured a photo of an embattled Berlusconi with an accompanying headline of 'The Godfather', which alluded to the well-connected minister's many personal and political woes, plus Italy's infamous Mafia.

Holiday retreat

It was with quite poetic irony that these fresh abrasive remarks by an Italian tourism official caused the German Chancellor Gerhard Schroeder to consider cancelling his annual holidays in Italy – a decision released publicly to the media.

Schroeder's threat sparked fears in Italy of a German tourist boycott of the country's balmy Mediterranean climes. With one eye on the diplomatic tensions and the other on the potentially disappearing tourism revenues, officials from Italian towns – which depend heavily on German visitors – called for Stefani's resignation. These pleas were, initially, resisted by the Italian government. The Italian government's opposition party also leapt upon the opportunity to make capital from both Berlusconi and Stefani's PR gaffes and the international discontent that their remarks had sparked.

Then, in an attempt at making personal amends, Stefani invited Schroeder to spend time with him during his regular holiday visit so he could prove to him that he really liked Germans. This was probably as appealing as having Hannibal Lecter inviting you over for a glass of Chianti.

The Italian government then issued a written statement distancing itself from Stefani's comments yet stopped well short of an official apology for what were the blundering words of a government official. But as widespread coverage of the comments increased international condemnation of the issues, Stefani, Italy's undersecretary for tourism, was forced to resign just one week later. A sacrificial lamb for the Chianti?

Leading by example

The man who'd originally provoked the spat, Berlusconi, had still not apologized for his 'Nazi' jibe of weeks earlier, although he initially expressed regret for having made it. However, in an Indian-giving gesture, Berlusconi backed away from his statement of regret, whenever pressed on the issue.

In a carefully worded – and intentionally ambiguous statement – the German government declared that it was 'assuming that the [apologetic] statements... represent the view of the Italian government and that they will not be revised'. This was a covert dig at Berlusconi.

A subsequent reprise of the two countries' failure to see eye to eye emerged when German ministers complained to the EU over one Italian winemaker's controversial range of tipples which includes an edition called 'Fuhrerwein', allegedly produced in tribute to Nazi leader Adolf Hitler.

LESSONS LEARNT

Much like any modern company, national leaders are seen as elected representatives who speak on behalf of a larger entity. Just as the deeds – and words – of those in corporate governance roles can have a bearing on corporate reputation and image, so too do the behaviours of international politicians. Sometimes, however, people in positions of very real power can believe that they and their actions are beyond reproach. But in the face of reproach, the skills of the PR consultant can be productively utilized to engender clearer understanding and a smoother relationship.

Direct mail – Volkswagen blasted over bomb mailer

Media spin:
'Volkswagen: the mailing campaign that bombed'

The Guardian

The Ealing Broadway terrorist bomb put London and mainland UK on high alert in July 2000. Therefore, when people began receive a mailer emblazoned with the legend 'Suspicious Package', alarm and fear for personal safety were heightened.

On discovering that the mailer was an unfortunately timed promotional stunt for Volkswagen's innovatively styled 'Sharan' people carrier, police contacted the Euro car giant asking it to halt the mailing. While explaining that it had planned and activated its direct mail campaign well before the terrorists had struck, VW ultimately declared that it couldn't stop the mailer's progress. Couldn't or wouldn't, sceptics wondered.

Despite the Ealing bomb having exploded on a Thursday evening, Volkswagen said it was impossible to stem the flow of 130,000 mailers which were churning through a direct mail processing house; nervous customers were still receiving the 'Suspicious Package' mail-outs on the following Tuesday.

Defusing the situation

Even after police and consumer complaints to Volkswagen plus lots of negative media publicity for what came to be perceived as a sinister attempt to create intrigue, VW's then press officer said 20 official complaints was 'not a huge number in terms of how many mailers were sent out'.

LESSONS LEARNT

When a company exacerbates public concerns (albeit unwittingly), it runs the risk of being viewed in a pretty dim light. The pressure is on companies to be magnanimous, responsible and indeed sensitive, even when unfortunate timing conspires to create tension. From a PR viewpoint, trying to bring a sense of perspective in times of alarm can be a good thing, but failure to express genuine empathy – if not take remedial action – at a time when national nerves are frayed, might be perceived as bad form.

Disclosure – 'Virus' catches consultancy out

Media spin:
'PR firm red faced over self-critical e-mail to Press'

Seattle Times

The careless use of e-mail technology landed New York PR firm Shepardson, Stern & Kaminsky in deep 'do–do' after it mistakenly sent journalists a candid SWOT analysis (Strengths, Weaknesses, Opportunities and Threats) prepared for one of its biotechnology clients.

As embarrassing publicity in the *Seattle Times* confirmed, the e-mail report included scepticism about and outright criticism of the biotech firm Cell Therapeutics (CTI). The leaked document was peppered with claims that CTI was very promotional and that it showed tendencies to over-promise and under-deliver with regards to its clinical results. The rogue e-mail also discussed one of CTI's most promising products – a new and much-hyped anti-cancer drug called Xyotax – hinting at the discrepancy between hype and results.

The release of such market-sensitive information looked to be highly damaging for CTI's reputation, as reportage of the SWOT contents was most likely to colour investor perceptions of the biotech firm.

Stopping the spread

Having unwittingly pressed the 'send' button, a frantic rearguard e-mail from the SSK consultant from whose computer terminal the e-mail had supposedly originated alerted recipients with an attempted scare tactic. The consultant claimed that the e-mail contained a serious virus and advised against recipients opening it. Unfortunately for SSK and Cell, natural journalistic inquisitiveness and the scent of a story proved stronger than the threat of a computer virus. Very soon, the word was out and reported in many prominent media outlets with consequentially damaging effects on the reputations of all involved.

Reactively, SSK released an official statement which – in textbook issues management tradition – distanced itself from any link to the problem and deflected blame onto a third party, in this case, a computer virus. But at the end of the day, it still looked like they were the ones who had caught a cold.

LESSONS LEARNT

Possibly the most disastrous dynamic to this PR gaffe was that in the sometimes speculative biotech industry, investors need to feel that they can rely on the professionalism and integrity of any firm they become involved with. And these qualities should be reflected in all dealings that any company has with its audiences.

Moreover, investors want to know that powerful treatment drugs have been extensively tested and are, in fact, bullet proof. The CTI SWOT analysis erroneously circulated via the e-mail blew holes in that premise. With the SSK report critical of both Cell Therapeutics' management and its products, and with several correspondents who had received the mailer discussing its contents, one investment industry analyst was prompted to suggest that if the SWOT document was ever circulated in full, at least CTI knew of a PR company that reacts quickly and appropriately in the event of a crisis, even if it's mainly to cover its own rear end.

Endorsements,
Ethics,
Event Management

Endorsement – Radio star makes waves

Media spin:

'Payola and the radio industry have been dancing together for many years'
ABC's 'Media Watch'

When Australian radio presenter John Laws found himself at the centre of a 'cash for comment' row over being paid to discuss editorial relating to several of his sponsors' businesses, he wasn't prepared to be picked off by media vultures.

Being extensively decried by the Australian and world media for 'double-dipping', Laws' best form of PR defence seemed to be PR attack, and he launched himself into the middle of a media mêlée. He appeared on prime time national TV show 'A Current Affair' and conducted interviews with the *Sydney Daily Telegraph* and several Aussie national newspapers. Laws came vehemently clean by admitting (albeit after he'd been rumbled) that, 'Everyone knows I'm a commercial animal, they all know that I get paid by sponsors, I'm a journalist, I'm an entertainer. So what's the problem?'

Talk jock of all trades

The 'problem' – which this Jack of all media trades failed to realize – was as follows. The public could accept that Laws was a commercial animal and one who, on occasion, was paid handsomely by sponsors. After all, they'd regularly witnessed him promoting wares in the media. However, most would be unaware that he was being paid to soft sell to them while he was in talk jock mode.

Maybe the public believed that when Laws was broadcasting on radio he was working for the radio station and not his private sponsors. After all, being allowed to command the attention of a sizeable audience surely necessitates some restraint, rather than flagging up topics that you've taken money to discuss. As someone who'd made a nice earning from spouting self-righteous indignation on matters of apparent public concern, shouldn't he have been walking the talk on matters of ethics and honesty? And as a self-professed journalist – on radio in this instance – was Laws perhaps expected to maintain at least a modicum of the impartiality expected of that profession?

Furthermore, if all of this really was 'no problem', why not simply declare the involvement with key sponsors before discussing topics relating to their business? Most Aussies would have reckoned that would have been reasonable, transparent and, as they say, 'fair dinkum'.

There is a very real problem when DJs get paid to covertly talk up their sponsors' businesses without anyone save a few insiders – in all probability PR or advertising consultants – knowing. That's why the Laws case led to a government enquiry.

The communications gurus who proposed and administered this 'cash for comment' campaign were in no way innocent. Whether in-house or consultancy, they must have known that they were crossing the line. But I'd wager that they and their clients were delighted with the covert coverage and endorsement they were getting from having a respected broadcaster discuss their business.

LESSONS LEARNT

Clearly then, this was a PR disaster which damaged the reputations of Laws, his radio station employers, the clients complicit in the subterfuge as well as the puppeteering consultants in the background. It was also an episode that brought the concept of business and media ethics – and specifically media transparency – into question. Secretly, most PR practitioners take pride in being able to covertly influence public opinion in a more subtle way than advertising or other forms of communication could ever hope to do. Sometimes this can be highly creative, although at other times it's just plain cheating.

When their strategies involve contravening media rules and guidelines then they've clearly crossed the line.

Ethics – The lie of the land

Was it really a Public Relations disaster when an industry-leading title published the results of its national survey on ethics within the PR business? Or was it an honest appraisal of ethics in business?

The *PR Week* survey, which canvassed the opinions of 1,700 Public Relations professionals, revealed that 40 per cent of them admitted they had 'exaggerated' in the course of pitching stories to media correspondents.

Twenty five per cent of the practitioners actually owned up to telling blatant lies on the job and a whopping 62 per cent of respondents said they had passed along corporate hearsay without confirming the accuracy of the information or the veracity of its source. Figures such as these reflect the propensity for 'spinning' which many are concerned about.

In further revelations, 60 per cent of PR practitioners said they felt 'compromised' in their work, either as a result of being lied to by their clients or not being given access to all the relevant information pertaining to a given communications task. Even with such damning findings, which suggest a covert complicity between clients and their PR consultants to massage the message, the *PR Week* survey concluded that all was not lost because: 'the issue of ethics continues to make the industry uneasy and many pros are even willing to embrace a drastic ethical certification process in order to salvage the credibility and reputation of their profession'.

LESSONS LEARNT

In an industry where practitioners do not need a licence to operate and are not governed or policed with any real rigour, what is the likelihood that voluntary adherence to a suggested code of conduct will result in a positive turnaround in the discipline's standing or ethical standards?

Event management – PROs left feeling sheepish

As exciting events go, farming and country shows are usually not top rankers, yet the advance publicity for the Royal Melbourne Show in the mid-1990s created quite a stir, at least in media terms.

As agricultural shows are representative of the country coming to the city, the event's PR team devised and arranged for a cavalcade of many things rural and regional to march through the city's main shopping thoroughfare, Bourke Street: a parade by all country creatures great and small.

While it's commonly held that people who follow the crowd do so as meekly as sheep, sheep from the Victoria countryside do not behave in the way their fellow flockers' reputation suggests.

Ewes take the high road

Never was this more clearly illustrated when – startled by their strange surroundings and also by all manner of pedestrians, cars, trucks and trams – the ewes, lambs, tups and rams scattered in all directions showing single-minded determination to lose their minders along with their reputation for compliant subservience.

The precision timing pencilled in for the procession fell by the wayside as harassed PR executives were forced to down briefcases and press kits to help round up their flock like suited-up sheepdogs.

In what developed into a highly entertaining mêlée for bystanders, traffic came to a standstill as the nimble balls of wool sought to evade recapture.

A yarn worth repeating

If the state's premier agricultural show had struggled to secure what's referred to in PR circles as 'significant share of media voice' in the past, it certainly had no such problem that year thanks mainly to the meandering sheep.

Most TV stations featured the flock's bid for freedom on news bulletins later that day, boosting awareness of the Royal Melbourne Show's imminent opening. However, the adage 'never work with animals or children' was particularly poignant for the day's events.

LESSONS LEARNT

Was this really a PR disaster? In terms of logistics management and frayed nerves things had definitely gone wrong. But maybe this PR disaster made the show look like a bit of fun? Given the extensive exposure and reportage gained for the event, it certainly outweighed the stinging, yet fleeting, embarrassment suffered by the PR stuntmeisters on the day.

Financial PR

Financial PR 1 – Share value takes a kicking

Media spin:
'Will Beck's give Man Utd the boot?'

www.bbc.net.uk

The renowned volatility of the share market was demonstrated when a flying football boot wiped millions off the share value of one of sport's most successful businesses, Manchester United.

The share adjustment happened after United's then prized property, David Beckham, sustained a head injury during a game. The problem was that the clash with the boot – which saw 'Becks' needing temporary stitches in a wound above an eye – took place within his own team's dressing room.

Infamously dubbed the 'Scar Wars' saga, Beckham allegedly sustained the cut after an enraged team manager, the gruff Sir Alex Ferguson, supposedly lashed out, kicking a boot across the dressing room where it made contact with the star number seven. While Fergie tried to play down the incident – though significantly he didn't once apologize or express remorse for his role in it – Beckham's advisers made great capital of the furore. They were possibly hoping to engineer a lucrative move away from the club for the highly marketable and sought after star.

The media also got great mileage from what looked like a PR disaster for United. Some pundits speculated that Ferguson refused to apologize simply because he had no need to. Whispers suggested that Beckham – the husband of one-time Spice Girl Victoria Adams – had provoked a volatile fellow team member who attacked and cut Beckham before they were separated by teammates. Perhaps to protect the other player, Ferguson stepped in to shoulder the blame and face the flak himself. Closed ranks prevented the real story from coming out.

However, the negative PR created by the apparent rift between the club (or its tough manager) and the trendy footballer star whose personal image and brand are estimated to be worth £200 million, saw shares in Manchester United, a listed company, fall noticeably after the incident. Beckham, whose own PR was almost eclipsing that of United as a club, was soon sold on to Spain's Real Madrid at the end of that season.

LESSONS LEARNT

The link between the behaviour of personnel employed by any organization and its reputation or standing is perhaps closer than ever before, and for one important reason: more intensive media scrutiny. In the case of Manchester United, a significant proportion of the club's brand value is comprised of the collective image of many of its star players. The worth of modern 'brand' corporations – like Coca-Cola, Nike or Man Utd – far outstrips the value of their material assets. So when one of these image assets (ie Beckham) gets injured, or threatens to desert the 'company', an adjustment to the brand value is only to be expected.

PR – the discipline that is ideally placed to take an overview of all facets of any organization's behaviour – needs to acknowledge that it is powerless to control every possible potential incident that may affect company reputation and share value. All it can do is be prepared to offer sound communications support aimed at repairing any cracks in confidence that occur and mending rifts in any stakeholder relationships in the event of untoward incidents.

Financial PR 2 – From sexual relations to investor relations

Media spin:
'PR man fired for insider dealing'
BBC News

An ex-porn star turned PR consultant who tried to enlarge his wad by using privileged information to acquire shares, discovered the perils of breaching regulations on insider trading when he was financially penalized at England's famous Old Bailey courthouse.

The City PR man, Tim Blackstone, was fined £1,000, forced to repay £3,000 in shares profit he'd made and ordered to pick up the tab on £16,000 of prosecution costs.

Having formerly starred in several blue movies including 'Emmanuel in Soho' and 'I'm Not Feeling Myself Tonight', Blackstone made the seemingly seamless switch from sexual relations to investor relations, following a stint as a financial journalist.

Despite his considerable experience, Blackstone claimed, when being prosecuted in court, to be unaware that financial information provided to him by his then client, Murray Financial Corporation (MFC), constituted privileged information.

But, surely, as one who had worked on both sides of the financial fence he must have been even slightly aware of the ability of financial media relations – and its associated press coverage – to influence the perceived value of any given share stock? If so, this should have alerted him to the fact that he might have been in a position of privilege or simple conflict of interest, even if by innocent coincidence.

Share of media

As their PR consultant, Blackstone was briefed by MFC that they were planning a takeover of another organization, doubtless with the intention that he would advise on how to develop a financial communications strategy that would best support their corporate objectives.

Prior to getting to work on the project brief itself, though, Blackstone invested in a clutch of MFC shares, also alerting his octogenarian mother about the opportunity to do likewise.

As MFC commenced a hostile bid for its takeover target – a building society – the firm's share value was boosted, probably with no small thanks to several mentions in the *Daily Mirror's* City Slickers' financial column.

In promptly selling his MFC shares, Blackstone realized a healthy profit of almost three grand, yet didn't seem to appreciate that his good fortune would be linked to an ongoing investigation into illegal share tipping, coincidentally relating to the City Slickers' feature.

Slick operation

The UK's Department of Trade and Industry was looking into allegations that two journalists working on the 'Slickers' column – Anil Bhoyrul and James Hipwell – may have been among a cohort of *Daily Mirror* scribes who were suspected of pre-purchasing shares in organizations that were about to be tipped in the editorial column. Commonly, an editorial mention increased the share price to the obvious benefit of shareholders new and old. Some opportunists cashed in their shares while the going was good. Even the paper's then editor, Piers Morgan, was under scrutiny over his apparently chance acquisition of shares in high-tech firm Viglen Technology, the very day before it was mentioned in the City Slickers' column.

A rigorous internal investigation by Mirror management deemed that the Slickers' columnists Bhoyrul and Hipwell be dismissed but that the editor, Morgan, was not culpable. Unnervingly for all concerned, though, the DTI was pressing hard for a formal criminal investigation.

Over in PR land, as soon as Blackstone was summoned to appear in court for his alleged misdemeanour, he did the right PR thing and circulated news to his stakeholder groups that he would be unavailable to work on client accounts as he fought, in vain, to clear his name.

On being brought to court to face charges of insider dealing – which he denied – he was convicted and heavily censured by a judge who seemed intent on creating an example to those who engaged in this kind of financial profiteering.

LESSONS LEARNT

This incident almost represents the flip-side of the much-publicized Martha Stewart case, where she stood accused of dumping part of a portfolio that was just about to devalue. Here, stock was picked up on the likelihood of an imminent price surge.

Yet it's a fact that the temptation to use advanced financial knowledge for personal profit is not completely new to the Public Relations profession. Even a former president of the PRSA in the United States was shamed and stood down from office after allegedly trading client company shares in the mid-1980s. But it seems that such high-profile embarrassments do little to curb the temptation within some financial PR circles, where almost every entity from banks and brokerages to mortgage houses and mutual assurance societies rely on PR support and representation to manage their financial communications and reputation.

There's no doubt that, as in most spheres of PR activity, a developed network of media contacts is a valuable asset for any consultant; they're critical for establishing and managing relationships with financial sector stakeholders. But when the network is abused for personal gain, it diminishes the standing of all involved.

Just as consultants involved in the sports and entertainment industries, for example, regularly enjoy free tickets and invitations to glamour events, perhaps some of those working in financial PR regard secrets and tips as a perk of the job? The reality, however, is that the sector in which they operate is actively policed to ensure that breaches of privilege are a rarity as opposed to a bonus. In this respect, there's even more pressure on PR practitioners to adhere to codes of honesty and integrity as well as to have a ready understanding of the laws that govern the financial services sectors. They simply need to know the rules governing their clients if they are to represent them professionally.

Blackstone's client's reputation was slightly sullied, but not as much as his own and that of the journalists who saw their livelihoods temporarily curtailed for failing to resist the lure of the lucre.

G

Goodwill, Government, Grassroots Campaigns, Guerrilla Marketing

Goodwill – Trouble brewing

Media spin:
'Starbucks apologizes for water flap'
www.foxnews.com

When the Twin Towers collapsed in New York on 9 September 2001, the entire city immediately rallied to support the victims and the rescue workers involved in the aftermath of the terrorist attack. The devastation caused was always likely to bring out the best in people, though it showed the worst, too.

Caffeine megacorp Starbucks metaphorically spilled a moccachino grande all over itself by making rescue workers from the Midwood Ambulance Service pay US $130 for three cases of bottled water that the rescuers needed to treat shock victims. Despite heartfelt pleas from the rescuers, Starbucks staff were unmoved, forcing the ambulance staff to dig deep into their own pockets to pay for the water.

Word filters through

Later, when the rescue workers had time to ponder whether they'd been overcharged they called, wrote a letter and e-mailed Starbucks to try to resolve the matter, but their attempts again fell on deaf ears.

When they eventually got to speak to someone after repeated efforts, they were told that such an incident could not possibly have happened and were summarily dismissed. Feeling more than miffed, the workers felt compelled to publicly air their gripe and so posted a précis of the incident on the Internet. The e-mail contained a suggestion that this upsetting story be circulated among friends and fellow New Yorkers to mobilize a protest against the coffee giant. Subsequently, many incensed New Yorkers began to call for a boycott of Starbucks' stores. Only when disquiet began to get vocal, did the coffeemaker even start to take notice.

Amazingly though, they did so only after receiving several calls from a journalist based in Starbucks' home town of Seattle who had picked up on the story from the Internet. When the journo's initial calls to Starbucks' Chairman Howard Schultz and CEO Orin Smith weren't returned, it seemed that the company's senior management were about as responsive as its store staff had initially been with the rescue workers.

Perked up

It was only after the scribe penned, and his paper ran, a story about the incident and word began to spread via the Internet and word of mouth, that Starbucks took this potentially damaging PR disaster seriously. It apologized publicly and couriered a cheque for $130 to the Midwood ambulance personnel involved in the incident. Starbuck's CEO Orin Smith also called Midwood to offer personal apologies.

The Seattle-based company then put its money where its shop staff's feet had been by donating free coffee and water to those involved in the rescue effort. It also made amends by giving several valuable items to eBay's 'Auction for America' and making a $1 million donation to the September 11 fund.

In attempts to distance the corporation from the mean-spiritedness of its staff, Starbucks' President Orin Smith pointed the finger at the offending employees saying: 'It's totally inconsistent with the kind of behaviour we would have expected from our people, so it has been very distressing to learn of this.'

Grind and bear it

But when you consider the way Starbucks' head office acted in the face of customer dissatisfaction, the staff looked to have behaved totally consistently, given their lack of empathy and general intransigence. After all, hadn't the Starbucks Corporation itself behaved less than impeccably in handling this potentially problematic issue? At every stage where it could have taken action to remedy the situation, Starbucks messed it up. First, it ignored the ambulance workers' many attempts to resolve the water dispute, then its top management failed to respond to a written complaint. Even when a journalist called to investigate the scenario, it failed to return the calls.

All of this simply gave the story time to percolate and brew up a storm of public protest. It was only after the issue escaped into the public domain via the web and the press that Starbucks' PR machine eventually kicked into action. More fundamentally, Starbucks' management has to shoulder some blame for not providing an operational system in which staff felt empowered to act autonomously, so that they could have responded more humanely to the rescue workers' request.

LESSONS LEARNT

It's always worth remembering that the reputation of a company is tested not by how it behaves when everything is going well but by its actions when faced with situations that have gone horribly wrong. How wise seem the words of Albert Schweitzer, who said that 'example is not the main thing in influencing others, it's the only thing'.

Government – Grave error in burying bad news

Media spin:
'Jo Moore e-mail a disaster, say MPs'
The Times

If PR is, by one definition, the management of reputation then it's equally true that it involves the management of information.

Experienced PR practitioners develop an intuitive feel for what constitutes a 'good news day' for a story. A good news day can mean a quiet day when any given information is likely to get a favourable hearing. Likewise, it applies when a story revealing less than flattering news is deliberately released to media outlets on a busy day, when it may get overlooked. And that's where timing – yet again – becomes of paramount importance in Public Relations.

Good grief

A communications adviser in the British government's Department of Transport demonstrated her nous for timing (some might call it her conniving nature) by suggesting that an announcement on the benchmark targets for railway improvements should be 'buried' by releasing them on the day of Princess Margaret's funeral. The targets, you see, fell well short of expectations. It's bad taste but a good call from an information management angle; busy journalists, hectic newsrooms, 'miss a day and it's old news' type of scenario.

However, when this adviser's suggestion was committed to e-mail, then leaked to the press, the advice took on a new and sinister dynamic. The press had a two-fold field day with revelations over heartless PR manipulators capitalizing on the death of a much-loved royal plus spotlighting the bad news concerning the rail improvements. In actual fact, the planned subterfuge backfired by causing more negative attention to be focused on the benchmark targets for railway improvements than would have been the case if they'd just been released 'cleanly'.

Deadly serious

As the storm clouds gathered, one of the consultants linked to the story was also credited with having previously commented that the World Trade Centre attacks were a good day to 'bury bad news'. 'Does their callousness know no bounds?' the media asked, clearly aghast.

Confusion reigned, but wasn't enough to douse the flames engulfing the Department of Transport, which saw its reputation – and those lame target results – lambasted in Britain's national media. Casualties included the resignations of one special adviser, Jo Moore, plus the Department's communications director, Martin Sixsmith. The department's press office was labelled as 'dysfunctional' by Downing Street which, in time-honoured crisis management style, distanced itself with a very long barge pole from the disasters that were rapidly banking up.

LESSONS LEARNT

Knowledge, in both the right or wrong hands, is power. For practitioners, the consequences of the strategy you are proposing have ramifications not only for the organization you represent but also for the entity that you will always represent – yourself.

Particularly for consultants working in 'politically sensitive' areas, there's a need to be circumspect about authoring documents that might be compromising. Ask yourself, are the internal stakeholders as 'onside' as we want our external audiences to be? If not, work out what needs to be done to address that issue, too. And finally, if you don't want to have a quote attributed to you, then don't say it and certainly don't commit it in writing. Perhaps handling PR at a senior level within a political environment should carry a government health warning: any indiscretion can seriously affect the future health of your career.

Grassroots campaigns – Boob job exposed

Media spin:
'Which are poisonous, the implants or the allegations?'
Cosmetic Surgery and Skin Care News

The potential for a PR disaster is never far away when public health is put in jeopardy. And for organizations involved in incidents of this kind, the road back from infamy to credibility can be a long one. Yet as one American healthcare company showed, even after punitive litigation and negative media coverage over allegedly defective breast implants it had manufactured for enhancement surgery, it's not an impossible journey to make.

Dow Corning had been found guilty of fraud for failing to inform the public of the risks associated with liquid silicone in implants. Some media commentators even drew parallels between the implants and the petrol tanks of 'Pinto' cars, which sometimes exploded in car crashes; a compellingly graphic metaphor to portray the scenario. In short, the credibility of Dow and its products was all but shot.

But in a covert fightback, it engaged PR specialists Burson Marsteller to devise and execute a grassroots PR campaign to swing public opinion back towards a more favourable perception of silicone implants.

The frontline

In their truest sense, grassroots campaigns are carried out by legitimate groups, working in the frontline of where the issues are being fought. Facing a welter of militant women's groups lobbying the US government to ban all breast implants, Dow Corning needed to combat this by planting and nurturing positive perceptions of enhancement surgery. So, Dow and Burson Marsteller synthesized a counter-grassroots campaign by creating key influencer groups that could redress negative perceptions in a covert but highly effective way.

A medical perspective

The second prong of their campaign involved the attempted enlistment of credible surgeons – medical experts who could help assuage any public fears over implants. By trying to enlist oncologists as tame media experts, the campaign sought to profile breast implants as medically motivated and not cosmetically centred. And it did this knowing full well that post-operative mastectomies only accounted for about 25 per cent of all those patients seeking implant surgery.

The plan's main thrust was to generate screeds of newspaper, magazine, TV and radio editorials broadly outlining that women should have the right to make up their own minds about whether to have implants or not. They also wanted to show that women were unhappy about having the decision taken from them.

For extra authenticity, they tried to find an ex-breast cancer patient – preferably famous – who was prepared to be an advocate for implants. Burson Marsteller probably believed it could best leverage coverage by highlighting mastectomy patients who had begun using implants to restore a sense of confidence. In taking this tack, the PR strategy aimed to win the sympathy vote.

The bosom of democracy

The campaign, featuring an avalanche of 'letters to the editor', extensive participation of local representatives in media interviews, plus ongoing liaison with local women's' groups, culminated in a mass pilgrimage to Washington.

In the capital, almost 1,000 women – trained, drilled and bankrolled – lobbied government to demand the right to choose. Cunningly, the fake grassrooters avoided paying the expenses of those 'demonstrators', who may have been required to testify at government hearings on the topic. If it looked like these grassroots campaigners were being funded, that would simply blow the cover. Throughout the campaign and also at the Washington get-together, media coverage began to increasingly profile the right of women to decide. From a position where almost all the coverage on breast implants was negative to one where the client was able to see almost an equal amount of reportage both bad and good, the campaign's success was obvious. And the ultimate accolade came when the FDA Advisory Panel Hearings recommended, after assessing both sides of the case, that the implants should still be allowed on the market.

From the initial PR disaster faced by Dow Corning over the efficacy of its implants to the eventual victory of the court ruling, the campaign showed that public opinion could be manipulated with a mix of strategy, guile and finance.

LESSONS LEARNT

Most media organs are essentially interested in one thing: making money. Most newsrooms, especially in regional areas, are considerably under-resourced, which puts pressure on local journalists to accept credible-looking, pre-prepared media information. As these scribes are often dependent on PR agencies for editorial content, there's an onus and responsibility on PR personnel and the companies that pay them to communicate honestly and ethically. But in the world of consultancy, the chequebook will win over this particular challenge almost every time.

Guerrilla marketing – Naked ambition

Media spin:

'Naked truth; police to quiz Vodafone chief over streakers'

Sydney Daily Telegraph

The sports field is an inherently competitive arena. Attempts to secure PR coverage within the sports marketing environment are equally challenging. But when international telecom company Vodafone effectively sanctioned two streakers – sporting nothing but Vodafone logos on their hides – to interrupt a game of international rugby between trans-Tasman rivals Australia and New Zealand, the game was well and truly up.

The stunt was certainly an eye-catching way of getting people to notice the Vodafone brand but, as with life, timing is everything. The two nude males interrupted a closely contested match in its critical final minutes. The streakers appeared when the New Zealand kicker Andrew Mehrtens was preparing to boot a goal that could have given his team a one-point victory with the seconds ticking away.

Barefaced cheek

It seemed the Vodafone streakers adversely affected Mehrtens' concentration as he missed the kick and New Zealand lost 16–14.

It was bad sportsmanship, overall, especially given Vodafone's status as an official sponsor of the Australian side. The barrage of media condemnation on both sides of the Tasman was extensive and heavy.

Even worse, when it was revealed that Vodafone had actually agreed in advance to pay the inevitable fines that the streakers would incur for their maverick stunt, Vodafone risked facing criminal charges for inciting and encouraging an infringement of the law.

Game plan

Having clearly been party to a PR stunt gone wrong, Vodafone had to answer some searching and embarrassing questions about its role in the debacle.

Head of Vodafone's Australian operations, Grahame Maher, denied that his company had been directly involved in the streak, but admitted that a man he knew only as Brett approached him the week before the game saying he might pull a stunt that would give Vodafone publicity. Maher told reporters: 'We said, whatever you want to do, if it's good for us we'd love to be involved.'

Given that Vodafone had agreed to pay any fines that might have followed the stunt, it must be assumed that the telecomms giant knew it could be supporting and sanctioning an illegal act.

Substitution

Vodafone wasn't prepared to handle the consequences nor the backlash from the streak, as its attempt to blithely shrug off the whole incident clearly showed. Eventually, Vodafone UK had to step into the breach to quell the disquiet, a lot of which was emanating from New Zealand where anti-Vodafone sentiment was running high.

'The incident is clearly regrettable and it was in no way any sort of official Vodafone sponsorship,' a spokesperson said, contradicting the fact that the streak had been sanctioned by its Aussie chief. The UK spokesperson went on to say: 'I'd like to think that most of our customers would not think that this was a Vodafone-arranged stunt.' He wanted people to *think that*, but it wasn't so in New Zealand.

Love your work

Just as the affair was beginning to disappear from the media radar, an Australian communications agency called Love – which coincidentally worked for Vodafone – decided to capitalize on any remaining media interest in the stunt. In an article defending the tactic in Australian media magazine, *Broadcast & Television,* a Love consultant, Monique Haylen, contradicted Vodafone's contrition, authoring what looked a lot like a self-congratulatory piece in support of 'Grab-Your-Attention marketing' of which the streak was an example. If you were a client facing all that flak, would it be helpful to have a consultant crow about its abilities to achieve 'cut through' via shock tactics?

LESSONS LEARNT

As well as subscribing to the rather uninformed 'any publicity is good publicity' model, Vodafone's actions suggest a dereliction of PR duty. You simply cannot be cavalier, careless or even clueless when dealing with corporate reputation and the image of a world brand. A brand is a valuable property and needs to be managed, handled and even protected on occasion. You wouldn't allow a complete stranger to compile your financial accounts, so why hand control of the brand image over to some bloke you don't know but who tells you he can do a job which just might land you in a spot of trouble?

Healthcare PR

www.prdisasters.com

Healthcare PR 1 – Open doors policy opens wounds

A Pennsylvanian hospital decided to improve its image by allowing the investigative American TV show '48 Hours' access to its wards in the company of the hospital's patient representative. It was thought that showing this person – ostensibly the patients' ally – at work would demonstrate that the hospital was concerned for the welfare of its patients.

Doing the rounds

Hospital management should have done exhaustive checks to ensure that everything about the hospital's operations was perfect, or as near to perfect as might be manageable, before opening their doors to TV. The '48 Hours' crew soon found surprises that undermined the hospital's credibility and damagingly reinforced a sensationalist editorial storyline, namely, that a patient must beware every time he or she goes into hospital. Obviously, this reflected badly on the hospital where the segment was being filmed.

At the outset of her ward walks, the patient representative's candidly told the reporter, 'I like to look for trouble,' and the hospital certainly obliged by delivering more than its fair share as the tour progressed.

Dead one-liners

One mother claimed that her son had received good care in ER but when transferred to the wards had been more or less forgotten. The only way to change that, she opined, was to scream the loudest, and her gripes were captured direct to camera.

Although the son was in no immediate peril, the mother's claim that he couldn't even get a set of clean sheets was a major vote of no confidence in the hospital. Every gripe and every shortfall was recorded on camera and into the microphone; simply unbelievable.

Critical condition

When another boy's mother added that she was deeply concerned to leave him alone in the ward, 'because I'm afraid they're going to make mistakes,' the hospital's reputation had lapsed into a critical condition. Then, compounding the escalating PR nightmare, the patient representative herself seemed to have her confidence shaken by what she'd witnessed. In an off-the-cuff remark to camera, she said, 'Families should be able to leave knowing that everything will be okay. That [the mother's fear] is awful to hear that. I really get distressed.'

In this, it appeared to viewers that someone who was close to the 'system' seemed to have lost her belief in its effectiveness and its safety. This hospital's wish to develop good Public Relations showed that it's neither the same thing – nor as easy as getting – free publicity. The programme illustrated the hospital's lack of understanding of all the factors that can influence PR to the good and to the bad. In this case, the desire for positive PR outweighed the skill and resources that can help safeguard the attainment of favourable media coverage.

LESSONS LEARNT

Of all the things to have gone so manifestly wrong, the hospital management clearly overlooked the most important fundamental in dealing with the media – be fully prepared. But you can never be fully prepared for live, unscripted television.

Perhaps more fundamentally, the management failed to grasp the TV show's motivation for wanting to do this piece in the first place. The media is rarely interested in showcasing 'good news'; good news just doesn't win ratings wars while bad news does. It also seemed that hospital management hadn't provided a rigorous enough brief to staff and patients to ensure they were all 'onside' before the TV crew's visit.

But all this overlooks perhaps the most common sense consideration: no one is ever really happy and positively predisposed when they're in hospital. Whether a visitor or a patient, people in hospital are more likely to moan because of the tension that the medical environment engenders. Any good media trainer will attest to the volatility and unpredictability that unbridled emotion can bring to any media interview situation. If the objective is positive PR, and not negative coverage that leaves an organization's reputation in need of resuscitation, be very wary of live television.

Healthcare PR 2 –
A bitter pill to swallow

Media spin:
'Pan debacle a PR disaster'
New Zealand Herald

When the taking of some tiny health tablets supposedly caused one guy to try and jump out of an aeroplane before having to be physically restrained, then contributed to another person writing off his speedboat in a serious crash, and had almost a hundred seeking medical advice, the consensus was that the pill manufacturers had some serious PR issues to contend with.

This was not an opinion shared, however, by the firm itself, whose most memorable and damning public utterance on the widespread health scare that the company's products had ignited, was that it did not owe the public an apology.

With such an unflinching attitude, it was no surprise that the incident quickly turned into Australia's biggest-ever medical product recall and the most damaging PR disaster ever experienced by any industry sector in that country.

Travacalm before the storm

It all started when Australia's Therapeutic Goods Administration (TGA) noticed a 'spike' in the number of cases of people experiencing blurred vision, agitation and a loss of balance. The common denominator seemed to be Travacalm Original pills, an established and trusted anti-nausea medicine made by Pan Pharmaceuticals.

Pan was Australia's largest contract supplier of complementary medicines and vitamin pills and was a prominent brand name in its own right. This meant that the total number of products that Pan had an involvement with ran into the thousands, under many different brand names and guises.

Trying to investigate the seemingly related illnesses, industry regulator TGA initially encountered delays in their efforts to access company records. While the company insisted that its Travacalm tablets were quality controlled, the TGA's independent tests showed huge variations – of between 0 and 70 per cent – of the tablets' compound ingredient.

With concerns over production irregularities and possible data falsifications, the TGA prudently issued a public alert via the media, instructing the public not to take Travacalm and other unspecified vitamins and supplements, until its investigations into Pan were completed.

However the media, in the grip of the terrifying excitement of widespread bushfires, relegated the TGA alert largely to a by-line or two despite the fact that 19 people had been hospitalized in the scare and a further 87 had suffered adverse side-effects.

Pandemic

Further TGA investigations at Pan pointed to the manipulation of laboratory tests on finished products and raw materials, false certification, the replacement of shark cartilage with beef cartilage, and inadequate safety testing of materials used in product manufacture. All from a company whose mission had been 'to present safe alternatives that people can take with confidence and trust'.

Pan rejected any culpability, opting to blame, and sue, what it called a rogue laboratory analyst whom it had sacked. However, this employee was counter-suing Pan for unfair dismissal while giving the media quotes suggesting that bad practice was endemic at Pan and that this state of affairs had preceded his joining the company. More damning for Pan, several of the dismissed employee's workmates voiced their support of these allegations. Several claimed that the sacked employee was simply following orders from higher up the firm's food chain.

Procedural searches showed that Pan machinery had not been properly cleaned between batch handling, raising contamination risks and the potential of allergic triggers.

Deciding it had enough evidence, the TGA called for an immediate public ban (announced via media releases) – Class 1, life-threatening – of 219 products made by Pan, suggesting that as it was a contract manufacturer to many more healthcare brands, more as yet unidentified products could follow.

With an eye on managing its stakeholder relations, the TGA also circulated a briefing letter to retailers updating them on the situation. Without wanting to bring down an entire industry sector, the TGA and Australian government nevertheless advised the public to abstain from taking vitamin and health supplements until the matter was resolved.

When 'resolution' came in the form of a total ban on Pan products and a six-month manufacturing ban issued against the company, World War Three almost broke out.

No panacea

With customary intransigence, Pan management stayed true to its somewhat frosty relationship with the TGA by slamming the ban and the revoking of its licence. Pan claimed that it was the victim of a witch-hunt in a desperate attempt to deflect attention from the real source of the problem: itself.

It seemed to have little sense of how to handle the threat to the company's own longevity, far less the impact that the scare was having on its own staff, suppliers, retail associates and their staff, not to mention any customers who might have been affected by the issue.

Pan stood by its his guarantee that Travacalm Original had passed all the required tests, yet this was somewhat at odds with the discovery that the 'uniformity of content' certification supplied by Pan was shown to have been falsified.

Pan's behaviour notwithstanding, it was the TGA – ostensibly the good guys – which copped most of the flak from there on in. In the announcement of the compulsory recall of 219 Pan products on a Monday – via media releases, stakeholder circulars plus the TGA's own website – the TGA's desired message was not being fully received or understood by its target audiences.

Of course, the updating of its list from 219 to 668 products just two days later added to the confusion caused by its initial proclamation. Pharmacists interviewed by the media claimed to have been left in the dark – was anyone really going to comment that they were delighted with the recall notifications anyway? – and retailers seemed unsure as to which Pan-related products were to be pulled. Many within these two groups said they'd be looking to the media to see which products were safe and which were not.

In soundbite mode, broadcast media only mentioned the market-leading products, which, while well intentioned, may have added to the confusion and misunderstanding. Some products were whipped off shelves in one store, yet readily available in outlets across the street.

Infection spreads

The TGA phone system buckled under the weight of trying to handle more than 300,000 calls in the immediate aftermath of its announcement, while daily hits on its website – which featured 'safe' manufacturers as well as Pan – exploded from a daily average of 500 to over 70,000. The media criticized the TGA's ability to get information to all key stakeholders, even given such unprecedented circumstances.

In the mayhem caused by uncertainty over the efficacy of Pan products, other interests could be criticized. Australia's Federal Government, for example, had taken out advertisements to publicize the dodgy products list, yet missed some key copy deadlines, which meant that the ads didn't appear in several editions of the newspapers.

An added complication arose when the TGA suspended Pan's man-ufacturing licence, yet Pan delayed calling a halt to trading of its shares, so enabling a privileged sanctum of key shareholders to dump Pan stock prior to its inevitable price crash. Again, those further down the information ladder – Pan's regular Australian shareholders – would be the ones who'd have to bear the brunt of this pain, simply for getting the information too late.

As the entire complementary medicine sector reeled under the crisis of confidence that the Pan affair had caused, the list of questionable products – ie those that may have been manufactured by Pan – swelled to well over 1,000.

LESSONS LEARNT

Where do we start?

If there was ever a contemporary case of how not to handle a cri-sis, this was surely it. Because Pan patently did not have a crisis communication plan in place, it shirked its obligations to almost all of its stakeholders and knowingly engaged in practices that led to the duping of many others, so threatening an entire industry sector with collapse.

At the core of its shortcomings was its refusal to acknowledge accountability or express contrition for any concerns raised by its own actions. Forget about 'rogue' employees, bullish statements about product efficacy and allegations of a witch-hunt; stake-holders aren't interested in excuses, they want remedial action. The buck for inadequate quality control, which potentially cre-ated consumer health problems, stopped with Pan.

Over the course of the incident, Pan had made many mistakes, starting with an unwillingness to cooperate with the industry watchdog. In times of crises, every organization needs allies, yet Pan opted for isolation. Then, when confronted with evidence of its own malpractice, it chose anger, defensiveness, finger pointing and wagon circling, none of which feature in best practice crisis management models. Plus, the information flow emanating from

Pan was decidedly fractured and this allowed other agencies to step up to the media plate and assert their own positions more lucidly, more cogently than Pan.

Pan's failure to keep its own stakeholders in the information loop, either via regular targeted communications or mass media advertising, eventually meant that many other interests began volubly attacking Pan's communications strategy. This, and a lack of leadership from an authoritative and available spokesperson, portrayed the image of a completely besieged company.

But perhaps the most critical failure in Pan's response was its unwillingness to express sorrow or concern. Just as Paul Simon believes there are 50 ways to leave your lover, there are an equal number of avenues for organizations and individuals to express regret, without necessarily admitting capability that could have legal or financial implications.

Interestingly, although the TGA had the power to clamp down on Pan early in the piece, it was highly circumspect with its own investigation, in order not to expose itself to the risk of liability if it acted rashly or prejudicially to Pan's business affairs. Yet this eventually damaged its own reputation.

Criticisms levelled at the TGA were that it had handled the entire health scare very badly, first by taking almost four months to restrict effectively Pan's ability to do business, and then by creating confusion by drip-feeding lists of products that may have been manufactured by, or had some kind of involvement from, Pan Pharmaceuticals.

While the TGA had tried to get its message out to all affected parties, the general feeling was that there was a lack of clear information about which goods were affected. Media pundits alluded to the brilliance of the Tylenol poison pill recall and its associated PR disaster management strategy. However, market sector commonality aside, the Tylenol case dealt with only a handful of product names, not a difficult-to-identify portfolio of 1,000-plus formulations and applications.

However, Tylenol's clear instructions to medical professionals to stop the supply of Tylenol plus the establishment of 24-hour helplines (as opposed to the Australian government's 12-hour version) could have proved useful in the TGA's communications effort.

While highly uncomfortable at the time, the Pan case eventually led to improvements in the way the Australian recall system works. The Federal Government was forced to look at setting down guidelines for new ways of labelling that clearly showed the ingredients and manufacturer, in the wake of the scare that almost brought about the demise of a market sector, ironically devoted to the promotion and maintenance of good health.

Hype – Bottled water launch becomes washout

Media spin:

'PR disaster as Coke withdraws "purest" bottled water in Britain'

With millions of dollars available to be thrown at, and made as a result of, the promotion of new products, it's inevitable that some run the risk of being over-hyped. Communications overload can sometimes lead to products failing to live up to somewhat braggadocio brand promises as well as plain old marketing 'puff'.

When Coca-Cola saw its traditional carbonated soft drinks losing ground as a result of consumers' preference for supposedly healthy 'natural' waters over sugar-based fizzy pops, its management felt the need to break into the UK's lucrative bottled water market, estimated to be worth more than £1 billion a year.

It launched its new brand of premium-priced drinking water called 'Dasani' in the UK, with a core marketing proposition that effectively boasted that the solution was purer than pure: 'As pure as bottled water gets', its marketers boasted. In doing so, it had assumed a product position that demanded absolute perfection if it were to fulfil its promise and deliver customer satisfaction.

Water damage

But just two weeks into its multi-million pound marketing launch, 'Dasani' was found to contain illegally high levels of toxic chemicals which, Britain's Food Standards Agency hinted, could lead to an increased risk of cancer.

As Coca-Cola executives reeled from yet another toxic poisoning scare – a previous one in India had seen its flagship brand almost banned under suspicions of toxicity – the PR nightmare escalated when it was revealed that the impurities were most likely to have been introduced by the firm's own bottling process in London.

As befitting a product that had been introduced to the public with an exceptionally high-profile marketing launch, the publicity accorded to its quick plummet from grace was commensurately high, and the damage to the new brand's reputation was severe.

Editorial coverage of the incident revealed that the source of 'Dasani' was not some ancient mountain stream or volcanic spring, but everyday H_2O supplied by local water authority Thames Water.

While the Dasani legend claimed that the water was subject to a complex, NASA-inspired purification process before having carefully selected minerals added to it, the amazing process was a form of reverse osmosis, which is used in many domestic water filtration units. More to the point, it was essentially the same mains tap water that was available to regular households in Britain's South East.

Water gauge

Journalists with a head for figures calculated that, with a retail price of 95p for a half litre bottle, Dasani was more than 3,000 times more expensive than the Thames Water used as its source.

Revelations of this ilk stirred up strong feelings among consumers of having been conned by the soft drinks company, also prompting the Food Standards Agency – which confirmed Coke's own findings that the impurity found in Dasani was the carcinogenic, bromate – to initiate a further investigation into the brand's 'purity' claims.

While highly embarrassing at one level, the widespread flak probably helped with Coke's voluntary, quick and responsible withdrawal of the 500,000 blue Dasani bottles that had got onto retail store shelves. The negative coverage possibly helped to minimize consumption of Dasani purchased prior to the product recall. This alone could have helped to negate some of the other disastrous fallout that can follow negative PR spin, especially health-related lawsuits.

LESSONS LEARNT

With Dasani, Coca-Cola had broken a golden rule of enjoying good customer relationships, namely, 'under-promise and over-deliver'; the company had done the opposite.

Pitching Dasani at the premium end of the bottled water market – against Euro market leaders like Perrier and Vitel – meant that consumers expected the very highest quality product: all communications strands, PR included, reinforced the quality message. Not only was the water nowhere near as 'pure' as the firm's marketing puff had bragged, but its impure 'spiking' had actually been caused by the company's own process of adding NASA-inspired mineral-enhanced properties to the H_2O. Understandably, consumers felt aggrieved when they got regular mains water that had acquired its toxicity – and premium price tag – only after being bottled by Coca-Cola.

Yet for all of this, Coca-Cola executives responded speedily and appropriately to the crisis by communicating clearly and openly, then acting responsibly. They candidly admitted that while the levels of bromate found in Dasani were twice the UK's legal limit, the water posed no immediate health risk to consumers and demonstrated a willingness to minimize any potential health threat by effecting a total voluntary recall of all stock. They really had no option but to do so, especially as they had to play down any suggestions that the poisoning scare could taint or affect any other products in the large Coke brand portfolio.

As the PR disaster unfolded, some Coke executives conceded that the prospects for the brand's relaunch were dubious at best. Others didn't think that the glass of water was half-empty at all, recalling the case of the French brand from whom they had intended to steal some market share: Perrier. Despite having bungled its own poisoning scare over 15 years earlier, the Perrier brand had effectively recovered its market-leading position in just over a decade.

Marketing gurus like Al Ries insist that PR is the most critical ingredient in developing a brand. Accordingly, any damage to a brand's reputation can only really be mended when PR is given the lead in determining how a company responds to the crisis it faces and how it expresses itself in the process.

As Perrier showed before Dasani, consistent communications can help consumers to forgive and forget; handled well, instances of reputation damage can indeed become water under the bridge.

1

Icons,
Internal Communications,
Interviews,
Issues Management

Icons – Home truths for lifestyle icon

Media spin:
'Is scandal soiling Martha Stewart image?'

www.abcnews. go.com

American homemaking queen Martha Stewart controls a vast business empire that markets a sizeable array of self-endorsed domestic products including towels, bed sheets and cookbooks. The Martha Stewart brand is an iconic one, built on one woman's squeaky clean, honest-to-Betsy image plus the supposed all-American values of product quality at great prices. Buyers deduce that if they're good enough for Martha, then they're certainly good enough for them. But out of the home and in the world of big business, these values eventually made a hefty rod for Martha's own back.

Homespun

When word emerged that Martha had fortuitously dumped stock she'd held in a biotech company – ImClone – just before its share price nose-dived, suspicions of insider trading were aroused.

Martha's timely disposal of the stock pre-dated the official release of news that the US government was unlikely to approve ImClone's planned new cancer drug. Martha's seemingly opportune piece of manoeuvring looked set to save her around US $220,000 but the ensuing interest in her alleged insider trading – selling or buying stock on the basis of private information not yet available to the stock market – proved to be of more serious financial consequence for Martha and her eponymous brand.

Of course, Martha's Garbo-esque 'I want to be alone' and 'No comment' responses to the media only made it look as though she really did have something that she'd rather keep quiet. Her inability to calmly assert her position meant Martha had failed to respond appropriately to a PR crisis. And during the trial itself, Martha's decision to turn up for her hearing carrying an exclusive designer handbag, estimated to be worth tens of thousands of dollars, did little to help if the aim was to foster sympathy for her plight.

Legalspeak

Maybe Martha's first, or second, mistake was electing to have her lawyers handle her response to the initial accusations. They vociferously – some felt high-handedly – denied the claims, vowing to defend her innocence. Her lawyers' decision to come out fighting made Martha look defensive and it flew in the face of best practice crisis management technique, which calls for a show of concern while appearing to be open and receptive. Additionally, the kind of language used by lawyers often fails to translate well when placed in media interview contexts.

Home truths

It seems the media loves nothing more than a fallen – or better still, falling – angel, so interest in Martha's case propelled the concept of insider trading into almost every home in the United States and quickly constituted a disaster for Martha Stewart the person and the brand. Shareholders in the parent company Martha Stewart Living Omnimedia were affected too, as they felt the fiscal pain of seeing the value of their investment nosedive in the wake of the allegations.

It's interesting to consider if there would have been such a high level of media interest in the story had Stewart not been previously portrayed as the epitome of perfection. Perhaps the perverse juxtaposition of the squeaky-clean image and the downright dirty deed helped to stimulate the ongoing attention of many media watchers.

LESSONS LEARNT

This scenario aptly illustrates the danger of building a brand on the image of any one person. For if it's based on a human being, it's only a question of time before that person 'slips' or experiences some kind of personal crisis or trauma which, even unintentionally, can have a detrimental impact on a company or its reputation. From a PR management perspective, Martha's advisers' decision to immediately surround her with a cordon of heavyweight lawyers was unfortunate. As soon as a lawyer speaks on your behalf, it looks as though you have something to hide, as is increasingly the case when a PR consultant speaks for an organization.

Irrespective of her guilt or innocence, Stewart's actions undoubtedly tarnished a home decorating icon, and to the tune of a lot more than the US $200,000 supposedly saved by dumping the ImClone stock. Her company was once valued as high as US $1 billion but the share-trading scandal wiped more than US $140 million from the books and its reputation has been immeasurably damaged.

Internal communications – Mechanical failure

A large American insurance company, Nationwide Mutual Insurance, ran an internal competition for its staff that offered two Mercedes cars plus a trip around the world as its top prizes.

But when the winning worker stepped forward to claim the booty the insurance giant reneged, claiming that it had only been joking. The company insisted that anyone would have known that it was not serious, given the triviality of the slogan-writing test laid down by the competition and the excessively high value of the prize. This cut no ice with the winner who decided to press for the prize, taking the matter to court where a judge also failed to see the humour that Nationwide Mutual had spoken about. The judge ordered the company to hand over the goods as advertised.

For the insurance giant, the pain of having to shell out a substantial amount on such expensive prizes was compounded by the unwelcome attention and negative press coverage that the story generated. The derisive publicity doubtless caused untold damage to the firm's reputation, but the internal disquiet that the affair would have caused among its staff and associates while the court case was being heard and reported on in the media, would have done little to enhance relationships between management and workers.

LESSONS LEARNT

Most promotions to external audiences have to adhere to legal guidelines that detail the exact terms and conditions of the promotion. Such checks can be useful for promotions aimed at internal audiences, too.

Interviews 1 – Losing the PR war

Media spin:
'Back to Bosnia to escape city thugs'
Evening Times

A housing association in Glasgow needed to assert its position as a competent manager of local council housing stock in light of attempted incursions into its territory by another, more predatory, association. It decided that some positive media exposure in a Glasgow daily newspaper would help it achieve its goal. Being 'financially challenged', the organization decided to handle the media relations effort itself.

Among its tenants were a woman and her kids who had arrived in Glasgow from the conflict in the former Yugoslavia. As she was deemed to be 'a special case', Cadder Housing Association had given her and her family emergency accommodation. However, after several years in Glasgow she had decided to return to her homeland. The association felt that telling her story to the press would portray them as 'knights in shining armour', so a local newspaper was invited to do a story.

A mercenary approach

When the paper's journalist and photographer arrived, the refugee tenant quickly asked what her fee for the interview was going to be, much to the surprise and horror of the green housing association management's PR, who had done no pre-interview preparation with the woman.

The journalist saw the predicament that the housing association was in and magnanimously backed away from the story. However, the photographer, possibly keen to win Brownie points back at HQ, reported the goings on to the newspaper's editor who quickly sent an investigative reporter to the scene.

The ex-refugee skilfully proposed a remuneration package for her story, including a pre-departure shopping spree in Glasgow's trendier boutiques and plush hotel accommodation. With chequebook journalism triumphing, she proceeded to relate her dramatic tale, telling how she and her kids were subjected to taunts, racial vilification, threats and even physical abuse while staying in the Cadder suburb of Glasgow. The gist of her tale was, 'I'd rather live in war-torn Bosnia than Glasgow.'

Splashed all over the newspaper, the story commanded sizeable coverage including a double-page spread that gave the housing association a huge amount of exposure, although probably not the kind it had envisaged.

LESSONS LEARNT

So what steps could have been taken to avoid this disastrous chain of events? Principally, an accurate assessment of the woman's suitability for interview should have been undertaken. A savvy consultant may have been able to detect that money was a motivation and either made a decision to drop the idea or provide acceptable recompense. If the decision was taken to go ahead, briefing notes providing the key messages that the housing association wished to communicate should have been supplied to the interviewee before the journalist's arrival. Then, an outline media release incorporating these messages should have been drafted for the journalist and photographer. Some consultants fail to brief photographers, yet the seasoned PR pros are well aware that a title's picture editor operates independently of, and sometimes at odds with, its news editor.

Despite all Cadder Housing Association's best intentions and efforts, the negative PR it accrued as a result of the coverage proved a major setback in its attempt to position itself as an exemplary housing stock manager. All of which goes to show how PR can be a minefield, whether it's in the former Yugoslavia or in Glasgow.

Interviews 2 – Dogged by bad publicity

Media spin:
'League star red-faced after rape joke'
The Age

When six Canterbury Bulldogs Rugby League players were accused of gang-raping a woman in an Australian holiday resort, the negative publicity generated posed a threat to their club's existence, as well as to the longevity of the football code itself.

With unfortunate timing for the sport, the incident took place just prior to the launch of the National Rugby League's 2004 season; just when the NRL was launching a campaign specifically aimed at attracting more women to support the game. For the reputations of all involved, it looked to be a career-threatening injury.

As the players all came from one club, the news was commercially disastrous for the Canterbury Bulldogs side. One prospective sponsor immediately withdrew its promised support and others considered suspending their commitment to the team pending police investigations. Media watchers and commentators pronounced that damage to the Bulldogs 'brand' was irreparable.

A Darren stupid thing to say

With the media hungry to pick up on every opinion, rumour and comment from those in the know, an unprompted utterance by one of the sport's contemporary legends added a new and unwelcome dimension of inappropriateness to the scandal. Darren Lockyer, captain of Australia's national rugby league select and also NRL team, the Brisbane Broncos, made the comment, just as the rape allegations surfaced.

On being interviewed at a charity rugby function, attended by a predominantly 'blokey' audience of rugby and Australian Rules footballers, Lockyer's bad taste quip could have, at best, got him a few cheap laughs. At worst, it threatened to cost him his place in the team he captained.

Lockyer told a joke that linked an Australian rugby legend, Johnny Raper, a stalwart for another rugby league team, St George Illawara, into the current controversy. 'You know, St George, they won 11 premierships with one Raper; imagine how many Canterbury are going to win', Lockyer told a stunned audience. Although there were a few laughs from the largely macho crowd, most people simply gasped at the insensitivity of the Lockyer gaffe.

While video footage initially showed Lockyer looking cocky as he prepared to tell his 'joke', he soon sensed the disapproving mood in the room. Clearly, his attempt to impress the testosterone-filled gathering hadn't injected the desired note into proceedings.

He quickly tried to brush off his remarks but when pressed by the media after the lunch – and made aware that he could be heavily fined for his remarks – he realized that a full-blown apology was essential. The code didn't need this other PR disaster, which Lockyer had just handballed to it.

LESSONS LEARNT

For celebrities, there is no such thing as a closed doors function. While Lockyer would certainly have 'known' his audience, many even by name, a joke that would probably have gone down well in a locker room simply had no place at a charity function.

In his role as captain of a national sports team, Lockyer was viewed as an ambassador and representative of the game. Audiences surely hoped that his views weren't 'representative' of his fellow players and associates.

'At no stage did I intend to demean anyone or trivialize the seriousness of events of the past few weeks,' Lockyer claimed in his apology, trying to excuse the error of his ways. But critics wondered exactly what the hitherto respected rugby star had intended to achieve with the quip, especially at a time when allegations of sexual misconduct and male chauvinist piggery were hounding not just the Bulldogs but also players from AFL side St Kilda and English Premiership team, Leicester City. In this, Lockyer showed a lack of awareness and sensitivity, but that can always be a problem for celebrities who tend to live lives somewhat insulated from 'public opinion'.

Strangely, rather than authoritatively denounce the insensitivity of Lockyer's quip, several of rugby league's opinion formers tried to dismiss it by claiming that it was 'out of character'; some kind of inexplicable aberration. Attempts to play down the gravity of poor behaviour may also be misconstrued as failing to take issues seriously, which can actually accentuate the damage.

In the realm of corporate or brand image, the behaviour of high-profile people in the media spotlight is a more critical determinant of public opinion than money spent on high-profile marketing campaigns. The media highlighted the disparity between the Bulldogs players' off-field trouble and the game's attempt to attract more female fans.

With increasingly intrusive trends in the media, including fly-on-the-wall documentaries, reality TV and undercover journalism, nothing less than 100 per cent consistency and 100 per cent integrity will support corporate or brand image. While this is totally unrealistic, there is precious little room for the slightest gaffe.

Lockyer's jape was a glaring example of public speaking amateurism; the failure to 'know' your audience and gauge its mood. That's why most sports stars prefer to do all their talking on the field of play; it's where they're at their expressive best.

Issues management – Pouring oil on troubled waters

Media spin:

'Coroner blames Esso for Longford disaster'

The Age

After an explosion tore through its gas plant in Longford, Australia, killing two men, injuring eight and leaving parts of Victoria without gas for two weeks, Esso Australia faced a real PR crisis.

The petrochemicals giant appeared to conduct its initial response communications well but the pressure started to show after a leading law firm was engaged by businesses affected by the explosion. This resulted in a $1.3 billion action launched against Esso. Observers noted that the tenor of communications seemed to switch around this point, with the Esso PR response seemingly hijacked by the legal eagles who had moved in to defend the lawsuit. Attempts by Esso's then head of corporate communications, Ron Webb, to appear empathetic and genuinely concerned following the incident seemed to be hamstrung by Esso's need to protect itself legally and financially.

Emotion fuelled

Consequently, Webb's stilted responses are thought to have been detrimental to the relationship between Esso's communications team and the media. Webb himself also broke one of the cardinal rules of PR representation, namely, 'don't take it personally', and he irked several media correspondents by attempting to influence how they reported the ensuing court proceedings. Webb is on record as saying: 'I just wanted to balance the kicking we were getting.'

When your company is at the centre of an incident that cost lives, disrupted essential services and affected many livelihoods, realism dictates that a kicking is what's going to be meted out, no matter whether it's intensity is warranted or not.

If the earlier legal intervention had made Esso appear a little terse as the circumstances of the case were debated, its decision at the investigative commission to blame its control-room operator for the explosion turned even more people against it. Detractors included the then Victorian Premier, Jeff Kennett, who volunteered his disappointment with Esso's internal finger pointing, deeming it to be entirely inappropriate. As a shrewd and popular politician, Kennett's pronouncement held a lot of sway and definitely influenced attitudes towards Esso, which found itself with few friends during the case. Esso's readiness to lay the blame on of its own was viewed by many as conduct unbecoming.

Esso was in a very unenviable predicament. The case necessitated handling the aftermath of an immediate crisis where emotions were running sky high given the severity of the outcomes of the explosion. Then, the launch of an official investigation also meant there was ongoing interest in and reportage of the case that fuelled the media fires already burning. Esso hadn't got off on the right foot with its strained attempts at communication following the launch of the lawsuit against it. Finally, a Royal Commission investigation into the incident criticized Esso's handling of safety issues and deemed the cause of the explosion to be in part due to Esso's shortcomings in training its staff to cope with emergencies.

LESSONS LEARNT

From a consultant's point of view, the ability to detach and separate the emotion from the facts is one of the most valuable assets in his or her armoury. 'Don't take it personally', has to be the media man's mantra.

Additionally, as the PR adviser can be an important mediator in the communication between an organization and its various audiences, any 'gagging' of this role undermines its ability to assist. As PR can play a key role in influencing public opinion, legal affairs staff need to remember that the outcome of court proceedings are not solely decided on the basis of what happens within the court. The company is judged by how it responds to events, and not only by how efficiently it attempts to close ranks and protect its own interests. In other words, is it worth winning a legal battle at the cost of losing the PR war?

Journalists

Journalists 1 – Registering disdain

Media spin:
'The Register's guide to controlling PR flacks'
The Register

The enmity between journalists and PR people has been extensively documented, with many media scribes snobbily dismissing the PR practitioner's valid role as a significant 'broker' of useful media information. There's precious little acknowledgement that the relationship between the two disciplines is a symbiotic one where, with a bit of mutual tolerance and understanding, the needs of each party can be met. Unfortunately the diatribe – mostly against the PR people who hold decidedly less power in the relationship – goes on.

Perhaps one of the most disparaging, yet eloquent, pieces ever penned about the journalist and PR person's relationship comes from an online news source called *The Register*. Hidden behind what we can only hope is tongue-in-cheek humour, it displays what borders on a phobia of PR people. If written by a PR consultant about journalists, you can be sure it would have been extensively reported as further evidence of PR sleaze.

As it is, with suggested abuse of journalistic position, advocacy of unethical behaviour and even malpractice, *The Register* piece, also posted on an online PR forum, doesn't miss its PR targets. Rather than document its various shortcomings, perhaps this piece should be allowed to speak for itself.

'The Register's guide to controlling PR flacks.'

Ground rules

First, understand that the 25 per cent of flacks who admit lying are the honest ones. The remaining 75 per cent are so hopelessly debauched that they're no longer ashamed to deny it. Those are the ones to watch out for.

A flack is a dissimulating pimp, and you are a scabby whore. Never forget this. They exist for the sole purpose of using you as a mechanism of free advertising. Of course, advertising is a valuable commodity; therefore, always demand fair compensation for spreading your scabby thighs. At a minimum, insist on interviewing them in your favourite restaurants, clubs and pubs; and under no circumstances spring for a tab, even jokingly.

Anyone who tries to place conditions on your use of the information they offer doesn't get it; and any journalist who permits a flack to place conditions on information is a spineless disgrace. Remember, you have the power of the pen and access to a readership. What you have is monumentally more valuable than any bollocky scrap of sanitized, market-tested corporate propaganda they might hope to peddle. Never let a flack forget this.

Quid pro quo

There *is* no quid pro quo; you hold all the cards. Therefore, never – never *ever* – thank a flack for anything. Flacks try to cultivate a fraudulent dynamic implying that you need them and that they supply you with something valuable (we mean other than free meals and booze), in order to bind you with the shackles of their illusory largesse. Never let them manoeuvre you into this perverse role reversal. You are the one communicating directly with the public; you are the one supplying the valuable service. You are the one on whose largesse their tenuous existence depends.

Therefore, expect them to thank *you*, and lavishly, for condescending to listen to their self-serving drivel. If a flack seems insufficiently grateful for your time, simply omit to cover the company he represents for a few weeks. He'll come around quickly enough.

If a flack ever dares to say, 'May I ask you a favour?' you should laugh heartily and reply, 'Of course not, you ridiculous creature.' Remember, flacks are obligated to talk to you. You, on the other hand, are free to ignore them.

Facts are cheap

If, under extraordinary circumstances, it should behove you to wrestle the actual truth out of a flack, your most productive tactic is always to consult the representative of a direct competitor of the company you're curious about. Flacks love to slag the competition and often have heaps more dirt on competing companies than legitimate information on their own, which tend to keep them as far out of the loop as possible (lest, in a drunken stupor, they should accidentally tell a journalist something he might wish to know).

Thus you get the straight dope on Intel from AMD's flack, the low-down about Ford from Chrysler's flack, the dirt on Trimble from Adams' flack, and so on.

To test the accuracy of such scuttlebutt, you must next ring the flack representing the subject-company, with a wildly exaggerated version of the dirt you got from his competitor.

For example, let's imagine that an AMD rep tells you that Intel screwed its distributors by secretly drop-shipping ten thousand CPUs to retailers last quarter. You then ring the Intel flack and say, 'I understand that you drop-shipped upwards of two-hundred-thousand CPUs to retailers last quarter.'

The appalled rep will almost certainly blurt out, 'Rubbish! It was barely five thousand!' Bingo.

Since the AMD rep is motivated to overstate the claim, and the Intel rep is motivated to understate it, *The Register* recommends splitting the difference and going to press with 7,500.

Lying on background

Whenever a flack is about to distort your perceptions with a particularly worthless, or egregiously misleading, bit of corporate propaganda, he will invariably preface it by lowering his voice and saying, 'Can I trust you with something... strictly off the record?'

This is one of the oldest rub-jobs in the book. The Great Cardinal Rule of flackdom is 'Never tell a journalist anything you don't want to see in print or on television.' They know perfectly well that everything they say is fair game; thus they bait you with such phoney forbidden fruits to ensure publication of whatever rotten titbit they're peddling.

Understand that whatever a flack offers 'off the record' is precisely what he is most eager to see in print. With that in mind, the journalist may decide whether or not to publish it, depending on his assessment of the relative advantages of either accommodating or frustrating the flack.

Tough talk

Once in a while you'll get some hotshot flack who imagines he can push you around. He might even try to show his widdle, and actually threaten to 'cut you off' from his stream of worthless lies. This is pure smoke. A journalist who gets so much as a whiff of this treatment should ring off immediately, and then conspicuously omit to cover the flack's employer until, after a few days or weeks, he inevitably rings back ready to crawl. It's advisable not to take or return his first few calls whenever this happens.

And do keep your hands clean. Never condescend to throw blows with a combative flack. Just cut him off, silently and certainly, and let him sweat. His supervisor will do your dirty work for you. Remember, his boss wants to see the company name in print, and will ride his ass mercilessly if they're not getting enough media coverage.

You are the gatekeeper – nay, the Saint Peter – of the great Publicity Paradise beyond, and every day is Judgment Day. Don't waste time scrupling over negative stories, no matter how much a flack might whinge. They're all secretly delighted to be in print under any circumstances. Never complain, never explain, and never apologize. Remember the immortal words of Brendan Behan: 'The only bad publicity is an obituary.'

So go forth, rejoice, and abuse your power relentlessly.

LESSONS LEARNT

The relationship between the media and the PR practitioner may not always be an entirely equitable or mutually respectful one.

Journalists 2 – Investigating journalism

Media spin:
'Globe columnist resigns, accused of fabrications'

www.cnn.com

Respected newspaper *The Boston Globe* faced a series of Public Relations disasters when two of its most lauded correspondents – Patricia Smith and Mike Barnicle – stood accused of falsifying editorial content and plagiarism.

The case of Patricia Smith arguably brought the most negative publicity on *The Globe*. Subsequent revelations about Smith's journalism career suggested that her 'creative tendencies' found expression in more than 20 columns where people referred to and even quoted could not be verified as existing at all.

The trail is thought to have begun as early as 1986 when, working at the *Chicago Sun-Times*, she wrote a review of an Elton John concert that contained many errors. When it was revealed that she hadn't even picked up her press tickets for the gig, the *Sun-Times* published a correction and barred Smith from writing for several months. It was bad news for the newspaper.

Time passed – along with memories of the incident – until, while working at *The Boston Globe*, Smith filed several articles that raised a few eyebrows, even among her colleagues. But it was only when a

Boston Globe reader officially requested that the newspaper review several of Smith's columns that the matter was given serious attention. As a result, all three of the *Globe's* 'Metro' section writers were warned about being able to substantiate story sources and characters. Clearly, the newspaper felt it had put Smith on notice but was still prepared to offer the gifted writer the benefit of the doubt.

Award to the wise

Within two years, Smith's somewhat chequered past was again all but forgotten when, in April 1998, she won a prestigious American Society of Newspaper Editors' Distinguished Writing Award for commentary and column writing. Around the same time, she was also nominated as a Pulitzer Prize finalist for her work. However, in the middle of her hectic schedule she put together four columns that aroused suspicions of overt invention, particularly one regarding a female cancer patient referred to only by her first name.

This time her employers were determined to get to the bottom of the allegations. After exhaustive discussions with her colleagues about her work and then, after the diligent checking of voter rolls to determine the existence of characters Smith referred to in her stories, the paper's Managing Editor confronted Smith about the issue.

Freedom of the press

Smith accepted culpability and was asked to resign, but was also granted permission to pen one final article. In this, she admitted to spicing up the cancer story and apologized to the newspaper readership, offering the suggestion that 'it didn't happen often' as a way of minimizing the gravity of the transgression. Her newspaper bosses were squirming with embarrassment given that her admissions undermined the very currencies that a newspaper is supposed to trade in – truth, accuracy and integrity. Newspapers depend on people being prepared to believe what they read.

To be seen as doing the right thing, *The Boston Globe* asked the American Society of Newspaper Editors to rescind Smith's recent award – which it did – and continued an internal investigation into her work. This eventually revealed that more than 20 columns by Smith included references to people whose existence couldn't be verified. It cast a huge question mark over the career of an otherwise gifted journalist and the editorial rigour of the titles she had worked for. This also made a mockery of Smith's final claims that such incidents 'didn't happen often'.

The Globe became further mired in controversy when it suspended another of its writers, Mike Barnicle, for two months for using material out of, and also recommending that readers buy, a book by popular comedian George Carlin. Those with an axe to grind against The Globe and Barnicle made great capital from the fact that the newspaper had sacked Patricia Smith, a black writer, for her offence but had merely suspended the Caucasian Barnicle for the error of his ways. And yet again, The Boston Globe was compelled to swing into PR fire-fighting mode.

LESSONS LEARNT

PR disasters will happen, but it is how an organization responds to a crisis that determines whether the damage to its image is repairable or permanent. Procedurally, The Boston Globe appeared to handle the Smith incident very professionally and from a damage limitation point of view – investigating, accepting responsibility, taking remedial action, communicating honestly with its readers – its behaviour was beyond reproach. Unlike that of a flawed employee who, even when given the chance to come clean, opted to present a creative version of events that seemed consistent with her previous work portfolio.

Journalists 3 – Smoke and glass mirrors

Media spin:
'Forbes smokes out fake New Republic story on hackers'
Forbes Digital

It was a publication with a 90-year long, virtually unimpeachable reputation for editorial insight into matters political and social. Its readership comprised politicians, industrialists, opinion formers, policy shapers and movers and shakers from all over the world. It influenced men and women of influence and was the in-flight magazine of Air Force One, no less. But when it faced charges that it was peddling lies, *The New Republic(TNR)* faced a PR disaster that shook the publication to its core.

Hacked off

TNR's lack of editorial rigour was uncovered, not by the magazine's own copy-vetting process, but by a reporter, Alan Penenberg, working for one of *TNR's* competitors, the now defunct news source, Forbes Digital. Stung by having missed a seemingly gripping exposé published in *The New Republic* regarding the ability of teenage computer hackers to bring US corporations to their knees, Penenberg began to dig into the story's background.

The piece, 'Hack Heaven', had been written by editorial young gun Stephen Glass, a flair-full, 25-year-old former Penn-U journalism graduate who had joined *The New Republic* as an editorial assistant, before progressing quickly to associate editorship. The Glass story centred on a supposed hacker, Ian Restil, who'd broken into the database system of a notionally prominent software firm – Jukt Micronics – and ransomed his way to a payoff of cash, a sports car and some porn magazines. The article also claimed that the new breed of young corporate crook was often represented by agents, hired to negotiate settlements with corporate targets, and one such agent was mentioned by name. The piece even fatuously claimed that government agencies broadcast a radio campaign to discourage companies from hiring hackers.

Glass half-empty

But these strands of the Glass yarn were almost totally synthetic, and none could be verified, at least by Penenberg's initial spadework. While Glass had not been diligent with his journalistic attempts to find a bona fide news story, he'd expended considerable effort in trying to cover up his deception.

Subsequent investigations into the body of his work while with *TNR* and other leading publications such as *George, Harper's* and *Rolling Stone* revealed his predilection for inventing situations and the people in them, generating fake back-up notes, creating false business cards for story sources and sending faux faxes and erroneous e-mails, all in an attempt to pull the Glass wool over the eyes of his editorial peers as well as the publications' readers.

For 'Hack Heaven', Glass even built a fake website for his imaginary software giant 'Jukt', conjured up fictional official-sounding government organizations and used his brother's mobile phone – complete with a voice mail message – purportedly as the high-tech company's head office number.

Glass-fired

With the website having been built on an AOL member's site and the phone message sounding suspiciously hokey, *Forbes'* Penenberg tried first to speak to Glass – without success – then approached *The New Republic's* editor, Chuck Lane, about his suspicions and signalled his intent to blow the lid off the scam.

Promising to investigate, Lane took just two days to fire Glass, after having endured further lies and protestations of innocence that included taking a trip to Bethesda, Maryland, the site where Glass had allegedly met Ian Restil and attended a national hackers' convention. But these facts, like more than half of the 41 articles Glass wrote for *The New Republic*, were built not on truth but on Walter Mitty-like invention.

On *TNR's* behalf and before his publication could be 'outed' by *Forbes*, Lane issued a media release admitting the story's inaccuracies and announcing Glass's immediate sacking. Reactively, the *New York Times* supposedly canned a Glass article it was considering publishing. Just in case. Two weeks later, Lane wrote an article aimed at trying to recover his magazine's lost reputational ground by asserting that for the press 'truth is... an absolute value'.

LESSONS LEARNT

Though it can be claimed that the majority of PR disasters are actually foreseeable, it's equally clear that a PR disaster can emanate from any facet of organizational life or any side of the media fence. And it can take the actions of just one individual to bring down the reputation of the collective.

Wherever they occur, most outbreaks patently fail to be policed effectively by professional, organizational, moral or personal codes of ethical conduct. As with cases involving other journalists like The *Boston Globe's* Patricia Smith and the *New York Times'* Jayson Blair, editorial fabrications constitute a violation of public trust and respect, and strain the relationship between publication and reader. Another school of thought holds that it's the reading public's taste for salacious, titillating 'infotainment' that has driven the evolution of a journalistic approach that's big on style and low on substance. And this flavour is distinctly at odds with reportage of the truth and the facts. It's exactly the same parameters that influence the desperate attempts at PR creativity, which can seem simultaneously 'cheesy' and deserving of media scorn.

While public opinion towards *TNR* was temporarily affected, perhaps the pain of the Glass deceit was felt most acutely among *The New Republic's* internal stakeholders, where fellow staffers who'd previously got along famously with the people-pleasing Glass became reviled by his action and shunned him as a 'worm'.

As a former copy checker at the magazine, Glass knew how to fox the verification system, and he abused the notionally honourable idea that journalists need to protect their story sources by preserving their anonymity.

Five years of law study and psychotherapy later, Glass launched a PR offensive, to acknowledge contrition and simultaneously promote his latest written creation, a novel entitled *The Fabulist*, based on the life of a young reporter who is a compulsive liar.

At least this time his source was, ironically, reliable.

Kobe Bryant

Kobe Bryant – Hoop star caught off guard

Media spin:
'*Bryant suddenly has a lot to lose*'
The Desert Sun

Kobe Bryant is one of the United States basketball's biggest stars. Lauded as one of the game's greatest guards, he's immediately recognizable as the advertising face for a myriad of blue-chip brands including McDonald's, Nike and Sprite.

More than being a good ambassador for a clutch of best-selling American brands, Bryant was viewed as the natural successor to basketball legend Michael Jordan as the new and fresher face of America's National Basketball Association (NBA).

In a sport filled with athletes who actively cultivate a 'bad boy' image that's compatible with the street-smart bravado many brands want to exude, Bryant seems to have always adopted a radically different strategy: that of a clean-living athlete. From the time he joined the NBA, Bryant was careful to mould his image as one of the game's good guys. Having married in 2001 and fathered a daughter, Bryant presented himself as a new kind of clean-living, straight-shooting role model for young black men.

However, the Bryant brand's image was rocked in June 2003 by allegations that he sexually assaulted a 19-year-old woman in his hotel room at Vail, Colorado. The revelations immediately damaged the star's brand equity and threatened the security of his coveted multi-million dollar sponsorship deals.

Many endorsement contracts feature a moral clause that allows sponsors to withdraw in the event of potentially damaging incidents involving the sponsored star. This effectively allows brands to sidestep any negative publicity that may be hurtling in their direction. The makers of chocolate treat Nutella quickly opted not to renew its sponsorship with Bryant, citing the abuse allegations among the reasons for its decision.

Disquiet among Bryant's sponsors centred on damage to the marketing popularity of a man whose number 8 jersey was the top-selling product in the 2002 NBA catalogue. Speculation suggested that sponsor companies were fearful that any bad publicity Bryant was experiencing could potentially rub off on their products or brands. After all, a sponsor organization's primary concern is to nurture and protect its own image first and certainly before that of any celebrity that it's associated with. And while some of Bryant's high-spending sponsors were concerned about the negative PR generated by the allegations, some continued to run ads featuring the star, even as the case proceeded.

Basketball court

While many assert that credibility and trustworthiness are paramount when it comes to 'celebrity marketing', many brands actively court the more renegade 'edge' of the sports stars who can give their products 'street cred'. That's why some of the NBA's occasionally maverick stars like Michael Jordan and Jason Kidd have survived extra-marital affair and wife-bashing allegations, respectively. And who could ignore the excesses of sometime basketball player Dennis 'The Menace' Rodman, he of the party wild man, affair with Madonna and drink driving reputation?

Yet public opinion about Kobe Bryant, previously seen as an allround nice guy, may not be so forgiving. The public feels somehow duped when someone they trust is alleged to have breached the rules.

Consequently, the backlash can be stronger than against someone who has always been seen as a rogue. While Bryant the person may emerge unscathed from the rape allegations, it will be interesting to see how badly affected Bryant the brand is in the long term.

LESSONS LEARNT

When the final klaxon sounds, companies cannot afford to ignore contentious and potentially damaging issues that could adversely affect their own image. In the world of corporate reputation and image management, consistency is of prime importance and perceptions are based on how a brand vehicle like Kobe Bryant performs in real life, as well as the ways in which the brand is presented in mediated communications including PR, advertising and marketing.

Launches, Leadership, Libel, Lobbying

Launches 1 – Unsinkable enthusiasm

Media spin:
'The unsinkable publicist'
Herald Sun

The PR requisite of resilience was never more ably demonstrated than it was by perky publicist Pepi Wells. Pepi's main charge was to build awareness for and promote the release of a glossy coffee-table book detailing the epic journey of the Australian boat 'oneAustralia' in the America's Cup. The launch of the tome, entitled *oneAustralia: The Power of a Vision,* was scheduled to coincide with the first stage of the world's best-known yacht race.

However, representing a PR disaster of titanic proportions, 'oneAustralia' snapped in two and sank just 175 metres off the United State's San Diego coast (where the race had started), rendering the craft unable to participate in the epic voyage. To many, this may have constituted a total PR disaster. But not for Pepi.

Undaunted by the fact that the boat – the book's focal point – was lying at the bottom of the ocean and so would not even participate in the race, Pepi admirably stuck to her task of book promotion. She remained upbeat with the kind of positive thinking that would have amazed Norman Vincent Peale.

When asked about the validity or futility of her task in light of the unfortunate sinking, Pepi said 'I think it's really good publicity,' adding, 'This [the accident] is drawing enormous attention to it now.'

So, what am I bid for a glossy coffee-table book about a boat that sleeps with the fishes?

LESSONS LEARNT

Topical relevance is one of the fundamentals for securing PR-initiated media coverage: your chances of coverage are better when the media are most positively predisposed to hearing your news. Timely topicality can help push an item to the fore of the media agenda.

This having been said, the PR push to promote a book devoted to the world's most prestigious yacht race was timed to coincide with the time when it was most visible in the public eye – at the start of the race. Unfortunately, timing has often been the downfall of the PR person, just as it was in this case: the PR person was talking up her product just as the thing was physically sinking.

The PR dilemma centres around the judgement call of missing a golden media opportunity or exercising restraint that might realize a more modest return on PR effort expended. It's rarely a fair contest.

Launches 2 – Creating media impact

The development of roads infrastructure is not a very exciting process, certainly from an editorial perspective. Nevertheless, there's still a requirement to communicate news of the developments to all relevant audiences.

In an attempt to bring some freshness to the standard media release efforts, one in-house communications team decided to let a new team member have free rein for its latest project.

Looking back on previous media materials, the new PR staffer saw that many roads development communications plans followed a template programme. There was the cutting of the first sod, councillors shaking hands wearing branded hard hats, female staff at the wheels of bulldozers, or senior managers driving road-marking trucks – but she wanted something a bit more novel and engaging.

She decided it would be of strong media interest to capture the precise moment that the road came into use. She planned to enlist a senior official from the council to turn on the new intersection's main set of traffic lights; that would at least get local TV, press and maybe radio out to do a live report plus on-site vox pops.

Lights, camera, action

Being a quiet news day, virtually all the invited media sent representatives. The idea of having the dignitary turn on the set of traffic lights certainly secured strong media coverage. For just as the councillor flicked the switch to activate the lights there was an almighty crash as a car – its driver rubbernecking the media event – ploughed into the back of the vehicle in front. TV cameras merely had to pan 180 degrees to catch footage of two mangled automobiles; one dislodged bumper even fell onto the road as if on cue.

The aim of widespread media coverage was attained. Most channels carried footage of the crash on the evening TV news while word of the accident was discussed on talk radio the next day. The ubiquitous phrase 'PR disaster' was liberally used.

LESSONS LEARNT

The PR person insists to this day that the flicking of the lights was not the direct cause of the accident; a claim later substantiated by both the motorists involved who confirmed that it was the large media presence, not the lights, that caught their attention. In retrospect, perhaps the cub's more seasoned PR colleagues should have seen the accident coming. A large element of PR activity is about control and certainly the management of factors that might affect or shape perceptions.

When you have a combination of moving vehicles, traffic lights and attendant news media you begin to see congestion, even if you're only reading it on paper. Maybe an alternative route would be better explored next time round?

Leadership – Conservative with a small 'c'

Media spin:
'Pouring scorn on "plonker" Hague'
New Statesman

The modern political arena is one where form is as important, maybe more important, than content. Many political parties survive or die on the credibility of their leaders.

In the late 1990s, Britain's post-Thatcher Conservative Party was suffering from an identity crisis. After seven grey years under John Major it was perceived as somewhat crusty, clinging to outdated notions like retaining 'the pound' as well as independence from mainland Europe. Within Tory ranks, it was hoped that a new head, William Hague – the youngest Conservative leader in a century – would modernize its stuffy image and help to make the party more appealing to younger voters.

Hague seems vague

There were problems with Hague's own image, however. He was widely held to be somewhat challenged in the charisma department. Accordingly, Tory PR and communications advisers tried to recreate the leader as a man of the people by positioning him in contemporary social settings and circumstances. The Hague PR makeover sought to re-work his image by revealing a previously unheralded verve and vigour.

To counter notions that he was a bit of a softy, his advisers publicized the fact that he had taken up judo and talked up his passion for cross-country skiing. The same kind of macho image had served Britain's Liberal Party leader Paddy Ashdown well, although Ashdown had actually been a Marine.

The ideal solution

Then, to target Britain's younger voters, the communications team facilitated an interview with UK men's mag *GQ*, which saw Hague claim that he used to drink 14 pints of beer a day when working as a delivery man for his father's business, supplying soft drinks to Yorkshire pubs. This was possibly one of the most ill-advised attempts to make Hague seem like 'one of the boys'. A sceptical media, which didn't believe Hague could handle 14 pints a month far less a day, picked up on the article and poked fun at him. The *GQ* revelations also drew howls of protest from several anti-alcohol groups concerned at Hague's apparent endorsement of irresponsible drinking.

The derisive media reportage that followed this interview far out-weighed any positives that could have resulted from trying to impress younger voters.

To cap it all off

Similarly, attempts to redress the public's perception of Hague as a fairly blonde character by having him attend London's multicultural Notting Hill Festival wearing an uncomfortable-looking baseball cap only exposed the Tory leader to even greater ridicule. Brits were used to seeing his shiny bonce and agreed with the media's summation that the baseball cap was a joke. Even marriage to Ffion Jenkins in December 1997 did nothing to dispel perceptions that Hague was somehow charmless.

Image in all the people

The notion that PR consultants or communications advisers can instantly 'do' an image makeover is tantamount to saying that you can simultaneously hypnotize 56 million British people. It seemed impossible, especially with William Hague. To Brits, Hague was still the tweed-jacketed teenager who'd been televised addressing the 1977 Tory Party Conference with a rousing right-wing speech. And the media frequently replayed that speech in a way that eerily haunted Hague and the Conservative Party.

If ever there was a case of first impressions lasting, then this was surely it.

LESSONS LEARNT

The creativity deployed by the PR advisers was somewhat ill-judged and may have actually compounded prejudices against a man who was unfairly pilloried for his looks, his monotone vocal delivery and a 'mummy's boy' image.

In trying forcibly to make him something he clearly wasn't, the media and then the public sensed a desperation that only drew attention to what were seen as Hague's shortcomings.

Libel – Lawsuit hard to swallow for PR people

Media spin:

'The most disastrous public relations exercise ever mounted by a multinational company'

Channel 4

The decision by fast food giant McDonald's to sue two environmental campaigners – David Morris and Helen Steel – who publicized claims that McDonald's was wrecking the planet and poisoning customers, has been described as 'the biggest corporate PR disaster in history'.

Rather than a disaster instigated by the PR department, however, the fiasco was driven by McDonald's management and legal advisers, keen to smite quickly information they saw as being potentially injurious to the corporation. But in pursuing David – and Helen – in Goliath-like fashion, the 314-day trial cost McDonald's more than £10 million in legal fees, with the editorial coverage of the court proceedings exposing the issues raised by the environmental campaigners to the full glare of the world's media.

Diet of information

The McDonald's court proceedings actually created a clamour for the information leaflet initially distributed by the pair outside one of the McDonald's London outlets, which the company claimed was libellous.

Entitled, 'What's Wrong With McDonald's – Everything That They Don't Want You To Know', more than 4 million copies of the pamphlet were eventually handed out around the world. A website about the trial, 'McSpotlight', featuring 20,000 files of courtroom evidence, received close to 100 million 'hits'. Additionally, a one-hour documentary called 'McLibel: Two Worlds Collide' was distributed via the internet, video and cable TV in the United States and at film festivals worldwide. In seeking to suppress information, McDonald's had accidentally promoted it.

Fast food for thought

So, what price corporate reputation? For all the money that McDonald's has ploughed into forging its image as a good corporate citizen, its overzealous pursuit of two minnows undid it all. Additionally, it's almost impossible to assess how the case has galvanized pockets of opposition to the US $30-billion-a-year fast food corporation, potentially stoking up resistance to McDonald's development plans for years to come.

While the campaigners were eventually fined for libel damage against McDonald's, it was small fries compared to the negative publicity given to the company for its alleged links to cancer, heart disease, poor worker remuneration, cruelty to animals and exploiting children in advertising campaigns. All of these topics were investigated and publicly debated as they came to light in court. Therefore, it was a pyrrhic victory for McDonald's, given that the firm is unlikely to ever recoup the damages or legal costs because both the defendants were unemployed and, therefore, effectively bankrupt.

LESSONS LEARNT

A real commitment to strategic PR – specifically, scenario planning – might have precluded what is widely regarded as the most spectacular and costly instance of PR madness the world of communications has ever seen. Because McDonald's failed to engage in effective scenario planning, the strand of Public Relations which scans the horizon looking for potential 'impacts' that may affect a firm, it failed to predict the media's voracious appetite for any juicy story that threatens to bring a faceless corporation to book. By trying to predict what could occur and making contingencies for some of the potential outcomes of the legal action, McDonald's may have better gauged the strength of support for the 'little guys' and revealed the very real health concerns held by many people about fast food.

Lobbying – PR hall of shame

Media spin:

'Exposed: Lobbygate comes to Scotland'

The Guardian

When Scotland opened its own parliament in July 1999, the hope was that it would mark a move towards autonomy, and signal an end to suspicions of 'English interference' in Scottish affairs. But when a scandal dubbed 'Lobbygate' erupted, it suggested that some Scots – most specifically PR lobbyists – were well capable of influencing political affairs north of the border in a way that raised questions about the integrity of several key Scottish government ministers.

It all started when a journalist with British broadsheet *The Observer* pretended to be a businessman interested in hiring the PR services of Scotland's self-acclaimed, largest independent PR company, Beattie Media. Essentially, the undercover operation involved secretly filming and audio taping two Beattie Media executives who inferred that their company held sway over several prominent MSPs (Members of the Scottish Parliament). Doubtless the deceitful dealings that the 'sting' uncovered helped justify the newspaper's own dishonest doings.

Who's your daddy?

One of the execs, Kevin Reid, an ex-Labour Party media monitor, boasted that his father was the then British Transport Minister, Dr John Reid, and that his contacts within Scottish politics were both extensive and influential. An inference from the taped session was that the country's top Finance Minister Jack McConnell – an ex-employee of a company part-owned by Beattie Media – was somewhat 'in their pocket'.

McConnell had formerly been employed for around six months with a sister company of Beattie Media, which he left after being selected as a Labour candidate. This company, Public Affairs Europe, had a fairly inauspicious business presence, though, with no clients and no turnover. Alongside the scurrilous suggestion that Beattie might have previously employed McConnell just so he'd eventually become their contact in the Scottish cabinet, another skeleton from another cupboard was that McConnell's personal assistant at the Scottish Parliament was also an ex-Beattie staffer.

Allegations aired in this 'cash for access' row, as it came to be called, included the claim that Beattie operatives could use their contacts to engineer meetings with ministers and possibly pencil dates in the diary of McConnell the minister through the ex-Beattie secretary.

The Observer revelations caused uproar, with McConnell vehemently denying the claims, other prominent politicos pooh-poohing them and Beattie Media first criticizing the entrapment campaign then apologizing to ministers for any loss of face caused by its staff's actions. The lifespan of Beattie's lobbying arm was sharply curtailed when Beattie Media appropriately suspended the activities of its lobbying division, which was quickly followed by Beattie Media's London-based public affairs partner, APCO UK, suspending all its links with the Lanarkshire-headquartered firm.

Despite attempts by all concerned to play down the allegations, the incident accelerated an investigation by the Scottish Parliamentary Affairs Committee. The SPAC was already set to review the role of political lobbyists to the Scottish Parliament, just prior to *The Observer* revelations. Although the committee eventually concluded that any MSPs (Members of the Scottish Parliament) named were innocent of any wrongdoing, aspersions were cast against Beattie

Media for the conduct of its employees and also the veracity of evidence given by several of them during the investigation.

LESSONS LEARNT

Pitching to win new business is a harsh reality for PR consultants. Certainly one of the ways to convince potential new clients of a consultancy's prowess is to demonstrate its record of influencing outcomes in a way that's in keeping with client objectives. However, when the claim is loaded with the inference that it can directly influence people in power, then ethics are compromised on all sides. Of course, when pitching for an account at locations of a potential client's choosing, PR people need to keep their eyes open for suspicious looking bags or briefcases with apertures pointed in the direction of the business transaction.

Beattie Media's own website once attested that: 'Nothing is more valuable to a company or organization than its corporate reputation.' Given that the 'Lobbygate' affair accounted for the closure of Beattie's lobbying division, the resignation of Kevin Reid and the besmirching of several of Scotland's top politicians, we might add 'political reputation' to that claim.

Mascots, Media Lists, Media Relations, Minority Groups

Mascots – Costume drama

Media spin:
'When mascots go bad'
BBC News

To assist with promotional and publicity efforts, many sports organizations have developed mascots: larger-than-life costume characters that, typically, reflect the organization's or club's heritage or 'personality'.

In-house PR teams, aiming to reinforce a club's identity and brand, frequently use mascot figures to entertain audiences and to add a sense of fun and light-heartedness to match day events and related functions. Usually clad in cartoon-style or caricature costumes, a mascot's responsibilities can include leading a sports team onto the field of play, handing out goodies to kids and 'goofing off' before games and at half-time intervals.

The mascots are also instrumental in attending club photocalls – kids love having their photograph taken with life-size cartoons – and spearheading community relations initiatives as well as local promotional drives to sell season tickets and merchandise.

Although often clad in exaggerated costumes, the mascot wears club colours and is supposed to be a friendly ambassador for the club and one whose behaviour is, at all times, consistent with the desire to create a sense of goodwill and favourable predispositions.

The beaten track

This wasn't quite the case, however, when two mascots from opposing football teams in England became infected with some of the simmering enmity that existed between the on-field combatants, Cardiff and Bury.

In the game's second half, Bury's home team mascot, Robbie the Bobby – who is ironically based on the founder of British policing Sir Robert Peel – donned a pair of boxing gloves and, much to the delight of the Bury fans, began to jovially spar with the visiting mascot, Bartley the Bluebird. Bartley, a strapping six-footer with a bright yellow beak, perhaps feeling more than a bit blue that his team was on its way to a 3–0 thrashing, couldn't see the funny side of Robbie's antics – because he smacked him square on the chin!

At least that gave the visiting Cardiff fans something to cheer about, many feeling that the Bury mascot had got his just rewards for his overt provocation. An incensed Robbie, feeling his dignity threatened, recovered enough to have a go at Bartley the Bluebird, the two ending up in a touchline wrestling match that lasted for several minutes.

Fearful that the fight could incite a crowd riot, Bury officials sent in club stewards to separate the pair and remove them from the field and public view. The bout was only stopped after the intervention of seven security stewards, which clearly wasn't an example to set for either club's younger football followers.

Subsequent to the fight and in light of widespread press coverage of the spat, both clubs sought to play down the incident. The Bury Chairman said that it started 'as a bit of fun until it got out of hand', and Cardiff City – patron of Bartley – responsibly stated their desire to 'establish the exact sequence of events in the fracas'.

While it was embarrassing for both clubs to have their representatives involved in an unseemly brawl – perhaps more so Robbie the should-have-been-law-abiding Bobby – no further action was taken against the clubs or the individuals under the costumes, despite the fact that Robbie was an amateur boxer whose mascot career included incidents where he'd 'mooned' Stoke City fans and ripped the bunny ears off Peterborough Town's rabbit mascot.

Panda-monium

Another sports club representative who was not so fortunate was the official mascot of Scottish football side St Mirren, who created two separate PR disasters for the Paisley-based team. Peter Panda, so dubbed because of the team's traditional black and white markings, first blotted his mascot's copybook when he enraged Queen of the South supporters (many of them from rural farming communities) by simulating sex with an inflatable sheep, directly in front of them. The act was a direct inference that the visiting fans were a bestial bunch.

After reprimands from his club, the media and the police, Peter Panda was warned to be on his best behaviour, as his simulation had tarnished the club's image and reputation. But at another home game, Peter the Panda pinched a team shirt from the visiting opponents' dressing room and, during the pre-game warm up, took the garment to the end of the stadium occupied by visiting Falkirk fans. In full view of the visiting supporters, the Panda proceeded to wipe his backside, notionally using the Falkirk team shirt as toilet paper.

In the mayhem that followed his act, the Panda was removed from the pitch and forced to explain himself to police officers and to mortified club officials.

In light of complaints from visiting fans and the threat of facing criminal charges for committing a 'breach of the peace', 'Peter' offered his beloved club his resignation, which was duly accepted.

LESSONS LEARNT

Although the deployment of larger-than-life caricature mascots seems like a harmless bit of fun, their ability to influence public opinion – and therefore an organization's image – cannot be underestimated.

As a mascot is usually a club employee, often part-time, his or her behaviour in costume or outfit can have a bearing on the club's standing as well as its stakeholder relationships. Especially when children are the primary audience for the mascot, the behaviour should be beyond reproach and certainly within accepted standards of decency and good taste.

While sports clubs throughout the world continue to see incidents where mascots challenge opposition team players and managers to fights, run onto the field of play to goad opposition fans or celebrate goals, as well as assaulting females while in club costume, the clubs will continue to experience PR disasters of this kind. Many organizations are now following the lead of corporations like McDonald's. It has a strict set of policy and behavioural guidelines for actors who play the part of corporate funster, Ronald McDonald.

Some clubs prohibit their mascot from being on the field at the same time as players, lest the temptation to interact becomes too compelling. Other clubs force their mascots to adhere to carefully choreographed and rehearsed public interactions.

A mascot can do much to create an atmosphere of fun and help clubs to develop the friendlier, cuddlier side of their 'personality'. However, due consideration must be given to determine exactly what 'message' your mascot is supposed to be communicating.

Media lists – List hysteria alert

Media spin:
'AMD tears up its PR plans after widespread leaking'

The Inquirer

The need for a long-term perspective coupled with a matching strategy is essential if Public Relations counsel is to work to best effect. A well-constructed strategy can help any company plan and execute the communications campaign that's required to relate to stakeholder groups. Confidentiality is paramount so that the competition does not learn of these plans and develop counter-tactics that may help it out-manoeuvre the original company.

Accidentally pressed release

So, when PR consultants for the hi-tech firm AMD inadvertently circulated the client's entire 2003 communications schedule along with drafts of some of the planned media releases to contacts on the consultancy's master media list, all the aforementioned premises went out the window.

This accidental release meant that rather than introducing one timely and relevant news item to carefully selected media targets, one unlucky consultant had managed to broadcast the totality of the year's planned communications effort. Needless to say, many journalists receiving this information felt compelled to share it with their own stakeholders and contacts – possibly including AMD's competitors – and this totally undermined the proposed strategic communications plan.

More than this, the information sent also contained details of AMD's new product plans and included somewhat ironic notes stressing how media releases were to be checked, re-checked and double checked before being sent to the media. It's a shame that the same safeguards weren't in place for the consultant's use of e-communications.

LESSONS LEARNT

Before you press that button, please stop to think.

Media relations 1 – Football guru's PR own goal

Media spin:
'Game's up for Hoddle'
Daily Express

To many, sport is the new religion and nowhere is this truer than in England where football fans slavishly follow their favourite teams, hanging on every word and syllable uttered by players or managers. Accordingly, attention on those who are involved at the game's highest level is intense and the media scrum – ever trying to win the readership game – is always looking for novel or entertaining stories.

Therefore, when the former England football team manager, Glenn Hoddle, unexpectedly aired his views on reincarnation, karma and disabled people while supposedly giving an interview about football to a sports reporter, the media had a field day!

Team spiritual

It transpired that Hoddle's quest to have his team play his version of 'total football' led him to investigate the 'spiritual' side of the national team's character as well. He had enlisted the help of a ' faith healer' called Eileen Drewery who used the semi-psychic laying on of hands to accelerate healing of a physical or emotional kind. Although many of the players were sceptical, Glenn's belief in Eileen was total, and some suggested that she had an almost Svengali-like spell over him.

In fact, when Hoddle started to relay his opinions on reincarnation and karma to a football journalist (topics not common in the rough and tumble world of British football), his opinions seemed to mirror statements made by his guru Drewery several months earlier. In his interview, Glenn uncharitably suggested that many disabled people might be working through some bad karma from a previous life and that perhaps their time on earth was meant to be a period of suffering. His views on disability and karma were an affront to most fair-minded people and a direct insult to disabled people everywhere.

A disastrous result

Glenn's assertions revealed all too clearly just how he had never quite mastered the knack of media relations – this was not his first media gaffe – far less how to make friends and influence people. In his time, Glenn had put a few journalistic noses out of joint, so there was a queue of people waiting for him to make a slip. And how the mighty fell!

LESSONS LEARNT

Hoddle forgot the basics of media relations: stick to the topic you should be discussing, repeat the two or three key messages that you need to get across and always, always keep the needs of your audience in mind. And as for the wise saying that 'if you don't want something quoted, don't say it', well that went right out the window, quickly followed by Hoddle whose tenure in the manager's job was terminated with some haste.

Perhaps it was just Glenn's karma for carelessly airing such thoughtless and hurtful views?

Media relations 2 – News release hits wrong note

Media spin:
'PR boss apologizes for press release about rock star deaths'

Ananova

It seemed that nothing was taboo or sacred when a PR consultant talked up the deaths of several musical celebrities, just to promote his client's products.

Consultancy proprietor Peter Noble, acting for the creators of the PC game 'Rock Manager', distributed a media release highlighting the suicides of Stewart Adamson, Zac Foley and Jon Lee, formerly prominent musicians.

The bow drawn by Peter was as follows: given that 'rock 'n' roll never dies' it's an 'ironic twist' that the suicides pre-dated the release of a computer game entitled Rock Manager. The game allows wannabe managers to practise putting together a band and steering its musical career. The next bow, though, was to the pressure of a back-lash from recipients of the media materials.

Noble quickly issued a statement offering wholehearted and heart-felt apologies to journos and the musicians' families for any offence caused by his spiel.

LESSONS LEARNT

Creativity should never be pursued at the expense of offending sensibilities, no matter the mindset of the target audience. The concept of stakeholder groups – *all* of those with a possible interest in your communications – must be kept in mind at all times.

Minority groups – Taking the message to market

The Queen Victoria Market in Melbourne sought to cultivate trader participation in its proposed new Asian cuisine hawkers' market. The term 'hawker' colloquially means that the food is offered at especially low 'sampling' prices.

The goodwill and support of locally based Asian provenders was essential as their endorsement and participation were critical to ensure the event's success. It was, therefore, they who were to be courted and converted in the first phase of the planned communications programme.

Scheduled to be held on balmy spring evenings, the night-time hawkers' market would deliver a riot of colour, exotic temptations and sensual pleasures, or so the internal brief suggested. Consequently, the in-house PR team sought to reflect these qualities in the tenor of its communications.

Colouring perceptions

In place of standard stationery, a more vibrant and distinctive stock was selected to convey the planned liveliness and flamboyance of the event. Text copy was written, then typeset and printed with no little expediency. Although the proposed mail-out looked great – to the eyes of the communications team – the response from the ethnic Asian stakeholder group was one of complete horror. Representatives from the offended group explained that the golden orange-coloured stock that had been chosen for the invitations was almost synonymous with that which was ceremoniously burned to commemorate deaths at burial shrines.

In short, the target audience thought that they were being mailed death notices.

Hue and cry

The communications team swiftly swung into reactive PR mode and personally called each recipient, painstakingly relaying an apology for any offence caused. This was not a simple or easy process, especially given that many of the provenders were non-English speaking and the communications team was not a multilingual one.

Miraculously, the communications team just managed to 'hold the press' before the information was sent to a media list of around a dozen ethnic news titles in and around the area. One can only imagine the kind of publicity that could have resulted from journalists receiving 'death notice' invitations.

Despite this initial kiss of near-death at the proposed hawkers' market, the prompt and heartfelt crisis management phone-round actually served to establish strong provender relationships and position the project as a successful and important local event in Melbourne.

LESSONS LEARNT

In multicultural societies, it's always important to be aware of the nuances of cross-cultural communication. Without this knowledge, it's all too easy for well-intentioned messages to be misinterpreted. In this instance, however, the most basic fault was to let the creative delivery of the message take priority over the audience for whom the communication was intended. As communicators, thinking about the audience before we compose the message can often help us to frame more appropriate – and therefore more effective – communications plans.

N

News Management, Newspapers

News management – Courage of convictions

Media spin:
'Justice China's way'

The Globe and Mail

When the PR propagandists of the Chinese government tried to prove to the world that dissident student leader Wang Dan was given a fair trial prior to sentencing, the concept of timing being critical in the communications business came sharply into focus.

Wang Dan was sentenced to 11 years in prison for counter-revolution offences. However, highly alert – and even downright dozy – media correspondents couldn't fail to notice that Xinhua, the China News Agency, managed to release evidence that Wang had been convicted almost before he went to court.

Wang's trial started at 9 am and by just after 1 pm he was pronounced guilty and sentenced with what could be described either as startling efficiency or indecent haste. Within one hour of the trial, Xinhua published a 2,000-plus word article, edited and translated into English, on its newswire service where the trial judge was quoted at length on the verdict she had just handed down.

Now, is that an efficient PR machine or what?

LESSONS LEARNT

Truly responsive, two-way PR communications is not universally practised.

Newspapers – Retraction drives newspaper bananas

'An apology to Chiquita'

The Cincinnati Enquirer

Most frequently used by journalists, the phrase 'PR disaster' is a label for any incident that causes negative publicity for an organization.

In the case of newspapers and other media outlets themselves, perhaps the closest thing to a PR disaster is where the publication makes a mistake and is then compelled to publish a retraction. This is where the medium apologizes for carrying inaccurate or misleading information that may have damaged personal or organizational reputations. Essentially, a retraction is the media equivalent of a product recall.

So, in 1998, when *The Cincinnati Enquirer* had to issue an apology to foodstuffs giant Chiquita Brands International for potentially defamatory articles it had run, there was a whole lot of humble pie to be eaten.

Unpalatable coverage

A series of articles by a senior staffer called Michael Gallacher, which not only questioned but also threw suspicions on Chiquita's business practices, were said to have been based on information offered by a Chiquita insider. Rumours stimulated by the article suggested that Chiquita had enlisted the help of the Honduran army to destroy a village called Tacamiche, that it quashed banana workers' unions and also endangered plantation workers by exposing them to pesticides.

These unsubstantiated rumours made Chiquita go bananas and the company responded with the threat of legal action against *The Enquirer* for defamation and – after it appeared that Gallacher's stories were most likely based on illegally acquired voicemail messages – charges of theft.

Because the journo, Gallacher, was said to have obtained – or stolen – the v-mail messages by deception, possibly with the help of an in-house accomplice, the local sheriff's department launched its own investigation, with Gallacher consequently facing felony charges. All of which damaged the newspaper's reputation among its own stakeholder groups including, critically, the advertisers that it depended on for its very livelihood.

Made to eat their words

Although its name sounds cute and delightful, Chiquita is not a third world cooperative with little commercial savvy, but a massively influential North American company. Its main man, Carl Lindner, owned the Cincinnati Reds baseball team plus his own bank and insurance company. The corporation was a big player. So when it began to lean on the newspaper, the latter had little option but to act swiftly. The *Enquirer* distanced itself from Gallacher, who had hitherto been well known for his probing, hard-hitting investigative journalism. The *Enquirer's* management declared, 'We can no longer trust his word and have taken disciplinary action against him.' Gallacher was suspended and eventually had his contract terminated.

The *Enquirer* then had to endure the ignominy of printing a large, front page apology to Chiquita two days running and posting the apology on its website. For a newspaper or broadcaster to have to publicly admit that it got it wrong is the ultimate affront to the notion of journalistic impeachability. As much as journalists love bringing others to book, they simply hate it when it happens to them. Additionally, there was also the small matter of the US $10 million settlement *The Enquirer* had to pay Chiquita for damage caused by the published articles.

LESSONS LEARNT

Unlike its editorial integrity in this instance, The *Enquirer's* handling of this potential PR disaster was beyond question: it acknowledged the problem, quickly put distance between itself and the source of the trouble, then was seen to take decisive remedial action. Acknowledging that the affair may have caused a crisis of confidence between the newspaper and its readership, the paper appeared fulsome in its assurances that it would redouble its efforts to restore any breach of trust caused by the incident. As this case so aptly proves, it's completely possible to save your skin even after a serious accident.

Off the Record, Opinion Formers

www.prdisasters.com

Off the record – All that glitters...

Media spin:
'What a gem of an idea'
Daily Express

Social functions, seemingly well removed from the cut-throat world of business, are hidden traps for the executive who lets his or her guard down.

This was perhaps most famously demonstrated when Gerald Ratner, head of the eponymous UK jewellery stores Ratner's, inexplicably proclaimed at a dinner function that some of his company's products were 'total crap'. Obviously presuming himself to be among friends, Gerald went on to assert that a decanter and glasses on a silver tray sold by his stores cost as little as a prawn sandwich 'but probably won't last as long'.

Gerald's loose cannoning triggered a volley of faithfully quoted media coverage which blasted a hole in his company's profits and made sure that its hitherto healthy brand reputation was shattered into tiny, imitation crystal-like pieces.

In the wake of the coverage dedicated to his PR gaffe, people simply stopped shopping at the stores. Eventually, the company was forced to change its name and Gerald was coerced into an embarrassing and humiliating resignation.

So enduring was the gaffe, in fact, that the incident has passed into everyday parlance, with comparable utterances subsequently described as 'doing a Ratner'.

LESSONS LEARNT

Whether motivated by the individual's desire to entertain or fostered by a social lubricant of another kind, prominent business people need always to remember that their words will be noted – and maybe twisted or turned – no matter the occasion, context or circumstances under which they speak. They must always be briefed or reminded that they are living, breathing manifestations of the organizations that employ them. If there was ever a salutary tale proving that there really is no such thing as an 'off the record' comment, then this was surely it.

Opinion formers – Image is a bankable asset

Media spin:
'Barclays has had a year of disastrous public relations'
The Telegraph

Brand experts make much of the need for consistency in communications; it's largely agreed that cohesion can help to reinforce the key messages that shape perception of the organization in the minds of the public.

But inconsistency down at Barclays Bank put things decidedly out of whack when the bank's advertising agency launched its new 'Big' campaign. Featuring British movie luminaries such as Sir Anthony Hopkins, Tim Roth and Robbie Coltrane, the impressive looking ads broadly talked up the values of aspiring to a better life. Unfortunately, the ads proved to be very costly and not just from a production value or celebrity fee viewpoint, as their launch and screening clashed with news that the bank was closing more than 170 branches throughout the UK and laying off loads of staff. The decision provoked fury both at local and national level. In fact, the ads catalysed a national furore with MPs, representing dissident constituents, voicing ire at the bank's lack of commitment to its customers.

Then, in a nifty piece of communications manoeuvring, competitor bank NatWest began running ads proclaiming that it was firmly against closing any of its branches. In doing so, it brightened up its own brand halo no end and simultaneously made Barclays look like the bad guys. And just when Barclays thought that things couldn't possibly get any worse, word got out that its new boss, Matthew Barrett, had been paid £1.3 million for just three months' work. The ads, the closures, the competitor activity and the boss's remuneration all created what might be described as an 'unfortunate juxtaposition'.

Reactively, Barclays put a plan in place to extend opening hours at the majority of its UK branches and, as a result, recruited close to 2,000 additional workers. Needless to say, the shelf life of the 'Big' ads was compromised and plans for a campaign focusing – more modestly – on bank products were mooted.

LESSONS LEARNT

It seemed that the advertising department hadn't consulted with their counterparts in Public Affairs which, first and foremost, suggests inadequate internal communications. Either that, or the management who oversaw all communications activity failed to spot how the ads might send mixed messages to the bank's customers. Appearing to spend squillions on advertising while cutting back on local and rural services – with the resulting impact on jobs, service and support given to many smaller businesses – suggested double standards. This was only likely to fracture Barclays' brand image.

The adage that 'actions speak louder than words' is particularly relevant when it comes to brand image. The most telling determinant of brand personality is how an organization behaves in the marketplace and towards its key stakeholders, not how much it spends on promotion or even how good it tries to 'appear' in these communiqués.

**Philanthropy,
Photocalls,
Political PR,
Promotions,
Propaganda,
Publicity,
Public Opinion**

Philanthropy – A good strategic fit?

Media spin:
' "Chocolate for footballs" scheme criticized'

BBC Online

In the highly competitive snack and sweets business, where product choice and homogeneity conspire to confuse the consumer, companies are always looking for new opportunities or initiatives to give their branded products or services some real differentiation: tactics that make their wares more uniquely recognizable and more sought after.

Such factors doubtless contributed to the decision by choccy giant Cadbury to launch an across-the-portfolio, pseudo-philanthropic campaign, which sought to give something back to the community, increase the attractiveness of purchase, build loyalty to the Cadbury brand and possibly increase market share.

The Cadbury 'Get Active' incentive scheme was simple: printed tokens on a range of chocolate bars were to be collected by kids and, thereafter, exchanged for school sports equipment. Cadbury believed that this campaign had a sound rationale with some very real 'value adds' that offered benefits – sports equipment – to schools within communities that were already wolfing their way through truckloads of chocolate bars every day. Plus, exercising such philanthropy would surely accrue some seriously positive PR?

Cadbury even secured the imprimatur of the British government's sports minister, who generously affirmed his endorsement by providing a few judicious quotes for the marketing scheme's launch press release. The minister doubtless viewed Cadbury's scheme as providing some measure of potential relief for his resource-squeezed department, which was struggling to provide new sports equipment to schools throughout the country.

Along with some carefully scripted *bon mots* from several leading UK sports stars, the confectioner launched its scheme to the public, trumpeting that it had made £9 million available to supply much needed sports gear that would help British school kids to enjoy a healthier lifestyle.

Sweet nothings

But while Cadbury had converted the government to the wisdom of the plan, a clutch of other stakeholder groups, who obviously hadn't been considered far less consulted at the planning and programming stage of the campaign's development, railed against the scheme, pointing out what they saw as some serious methodological defects. First up to bat was the Food Commission, which blasted the scheme as being absurd and contradictory. 'You can't get fit by eating more chocolate,' was their point.

In a damning article published in *Food Magazine*, the Food Commission pointed out that by the promotion's end, British school kids, many already struggling with the early onset of obesity, would have to chomp their way through 2 million kilos of fat and consume more than 36 billion calories.

The Food Commission also highlighted a major contradiction within government, where the Department of Health was on a drive to educate kids about developing healthy eating habits, only for the sports minister to condone a contrary marketing scheme promoting the consumption of junk food.

Choc-a-blocked

Then, the Consumers' Association expressed its concern, condemning Cadbury's corporate exploitation of children as 'nothing short of a scandal' before asking the government to withdraw its support and conduct a more thorough evaluation of the scheme and to more robustly police marketing schemes of the Cadbury ilk.

Influential British broadsheet, *The Guardian*, was one of several newspapers only too happy to expand on most of these themes, publishing statistics claiming that a child would have to consume 320 chocolate bars to get a volleyball, 2,730 bars to get a cricket set and a whopping 5,440 bars for a set of volleyball posts. Other figures suggested that a 10-year-old saving his wrappers for a basketball would have to play the game for 90 hours just to burn off the calories consumed by eating the chocolate.

With the National Union of Teachers also joining the fray to scotch the campaign, and signalling their determination to block the scheme, Cadbury was caught on the back foot. Yet it gamely insisted that the 'Get Active' campaign wasn't designed to make children single-handedly eat huge amounts of chocolate bars to get sports gear.

But the company was further challenged over a statement contained in one of its press releases that 'Chocolate is there to be enjoyed and can form the basis of a balanced diet'. It was forced to recant and rephrase to: 'Chocolate is there to be enjoyed in moderation as part of a balanced diet'. Clearly, the response to the promotion hadn't been as sweet as Cadbury would have liked and much of the mud being slung at Cadbury, stuck.

LESSONS LEARNT

One of the key benefits of involving PR personnel in the development of any kind of communications campaign is that they are usually able to assess the likely impact to reputation that will be caused by any communications-related initiatives.

Compared to those with a purely marketing mindset, for example, seasoned PR strategists will take into consideration the possible responses of all interested stakeholder groups, as opposed to just the market segments affected by the activity. Usually at the planning stage of any campaign's development, PR can help to identify all those groups who may react to the scheduled activity. If appropriate, PR can initiate dialogue that can smooth out and resolve any issues, so stopping them entering the 'public' – ie the media – domain.

With so many dissenters decrying Cadbury's 'Get Active' campaign, it seemed that very little pre-campaign stakeholder 'soundings' had been conducted. Pre-campaign feedback from these groups could have minimized the adverse reaction that the campaign provoked, so ensuring that the actual launch received a more favourable reception.

Despite opposition to the scheme, initial research suggested that the promotion had attained a modest rise in market share since the campaign's mid-2003 launch. However, the confectioner elected to appoint international PR company, Fleishman-Hillard, as a minder to its global reputation, in the wake of the criticism it experienced over this and other campaigns.

Photocalls – Hotel reservations over photocall

Media spin:
'Sexy secrets of kinky hotel'

The Sun

As a new addition to the Glasgow hotel scene, The Brunswick Merchant City was seriously struggling both with occupancy rates and general awareness of its existence.

The trendy hotel's original owners had initially tried to be 'niche' – appealing to a lifestyle elite – but had failed. With extremely limited funds to commit to communications, it engaged a fledgling PR firm to boost its profile. The PR activity needed to communicate that the hotel was a venue for customers of all kinds so, via a proposed media photocall, the PR team decided to show the various strange items that guests had left behind in the hotel rooms, to demonstrate its varied clientele.

With no time to engage long-lead media, a photocall was arranged for Scottish national and Glasgow local papers. It was hoped that the story would make the UK national editions of several England-based dailies, plus encourage imminent travellers to put the hotel on their accommodation shortlist.

Propped up

The photocall featured an attractive female receptionist, with a variety of props including two Doberman Pinscher pups, a huge salmon, theatre binoculars, sports equipment and even a garden gnome all similar to those which had been left in rooms. Photographers from most leading titles attended as did a reporter from the infamous tabloid *The Sun*. As the PR exec managed the photocall logistics, *The Sun* hack apparently disappeared into the hotel to speak directly to staff.

In subsequent coverage, *The Sun* went to town with a story whose theme was 'Sexy Secrets of Kinky Hotel'. The piece detailed how a male guest had handcuffed himself to a balustrade in the mezzanine penthouse, wearing nothing but ladies pants, suspenders and stockings. He had then accidentally kicked the handcuff key off the landing to the floor downstairs. His calls for help, which upset other guests, were eventually answered by hotel staff. *The Sun* used the PR's arranged photo, though favoured the tale that was probably sourced from an indiscreet – or short of cash – hotel staffer. While The Brunswick did receive positive publicity in several other titles after the photocall, the client's viewpoint was coloured by the inappropriate coverage that had appeared in *The Sun*.

LESSONS LEARNT

In devising a creatively eye-catching photo opportunity, the PR firm managed to secure exposure on a very limited budget for the hotel. But it had patently failed to cover all the necessary bases. The most glaring error was neglecting to adequately brief hotel staff against discussing any aspect of the hotel's business with any attendant media, unless sanctioned to do so by the PRO. And although the consultant claimed to have provided this brief, he had given it to the hotel owner who was already overwhelmed with hotel management duties and who probably failed to relay the message to staff. Irrespective of the event only being intended for photographers, the prospect of a rogue reporter turning up should have been properly planned for.

Political PR – Battle for hearts and minds

Media spin:

'What did you do in the war, Alastair?'

The Economist

The concept of PR 'spin' is thought to have originated – and still crops up most regularly – in the political world, where government communications advisers appear preoccupied with putting the best possible gloss on any story.

In the UK's Labour government, the man dubbed the 'king of spin' was the Prime Minister's former director of communications, Alastair Campbell, who has found himself at the centre of several scandals involving suggestions of spin.

Gathering ammunition

One of the most serious of these instances surrounded the validity of the government's rationale for entering into the conflict with Iraq in 2003. When the allies failed to immediately root out weapons of mass destruction (WMD), the principal reason for invading – or liberating – the Middle Eastern country was weakened and protests against the military mobilization became more voluble.

To assuage growing public disquiet the world over, Prime Minister Tony Blair revealed that a high-level 'intelligence dossier' provided all the requisite justification. But it did little for Downing Street or its communications unit's credibility when chunks of the document looked to have been culled from a 12-year-old PhD dissertation by a 29-year-old Iraqi-American named Ibrahim al-Marishi. Ibrahim's work had been cribbed so faithfully that it included uncorrected typos copied verbatim into the 'intelligence dossier' justifying the war. Even worse, annotated changes showing comments made by communications unit staffers were unearthed from the document's software code.

Controversially, the BBC suggested that the 'intelligence dossier' had also been 'sexed up' by Alistair Campbell who had allegedly felt it necessary to make the case against Saddam Hussein's repressive regime appear more compelling.

Collateral damage

Criticism of the British government's advisers became more sombre when a top British weapons expert, Dr David Kelly, committed suicide after being implicated as a possible whistleblower who'd tipped the BBC off about the 'dossier'.

PR now appeared to have been instrumental in the execution of seriously underhand dealings and was held to be implicated in helping to fabricate enough evidence to start a war and drive a troubled scientist to take his own life.

The British government didn't come out of the affair unscathed either, with Tony Blair's popularity plummeting in the wake of the scandal and many of his ministers and advisers trooped out before a Parliamentary Commission into the scandal.

LESSONS LEARNT

Communications and PR personnel are often caught between a rock and a hard place. While their speciality is to help shape and relay information so that it is palatable for media consumption, they are often pilloried for 'dressing up' information in a way that best reflects the organizations they represent. But can the media really claim that it never sexes up information itself? The information that's accessible through the mass media is rarely pure or uncontaminated, prey as it is to the commercial or political agendas of media owners and managers. For any form of communications mediated either by journalists or PR personnel, the words of Samuel Butler ring equally true: 'The public buys its opinions as it buys its meat or takes in its milk, on the principle that it is cheaper to do this than to keep a cow. So it is, but the milk is more likely to be watered.'

Promotions – Operating in a PR vacuum

Possibly the world's greatest promotional flop – with all the attendant PR woes – came in 1993 when leading appliance manufacturer Hoover promised free flights to the United States for its UK customers who spent £100 or more on a new Hoover vacuum cleaner.

With return flights to the United States normally costing around £300, droves of value-conscious Brits bought Hoovers even though they didn't want or need them, just to cash in on the flight deal. In terms of public response, the flight promotion was a runaway success with more than 200,000 applicants.

Wing and a prayer

Hoover's brand awareness was at its highest ever altitude, yet public and media hostility towards the company ran at equally lofty levels. Because of the overwhelming response levels, satisfactory delivery of flights proved highly problematic and, in practice, almost impossible. The exercise turned out to be an unmitigated disaster as the company and its airline partner failed to keep pace with – and honour – the mammoth and obviously unexpected demand.

The negative publicity suffered by the company, which naturally endured just as long as people failed to get the flights they wanted, eventually led to the company's loss of operating independence, but not before the sacrifice of three high-flying senior managers and £48 million needed to buy additional flights to meet the demand created by the promotion.

LESSONS LEARNT

The Hoover promotion was widely shot down as one of the biggest PR disasters ever encountered by a household brand. Yet surely this promo deal was as much a backstage mathematical blunder – and financial management disaster – as it was a PR one? Many people mistakenly confuse PR and promotions, but it would appear that scant consideration was given to the former when Hoover was planning the promotion to end all promotions. Or was it a just a promotion to end all companies?

Propaganda – Truth is the first casualty of PR war

Media spin:

'War atrocity propaganda exposed'
Institute for Historical Review

From its inception, Public Relations has been inextricably linked to the concept of propaganda which is, by definition, the forceful mass communication of a particular doctrine or ideal.

Propaganda developed by the earliest PR practitioners was used to consolidate and galvanize nations throughout the First and Second World Wars and contemporarily, international PR gurus Hill & Knowlton helped to devise and disseminate a new form of propaganda in the first Gulf War. The Hill & Knowlton war effort was simultaneously responsible for turning the tide of public opinion against Iraq, towards the US's resolve for participation in the conflict and, latterly, against the credibility and trustworthiness of the Public Relations profession.

The war effort

Public opinion on George Bush (Snr's) pro-war Gulf policy had been seriously divided, with almost half of all Americans wanting Bush to hold back from committing US troops to conflict. To tip public opinion in favour of military mobilization, Hill & Knowlton was enlisted to build backing for a war against Iraq. H&K's campaign and consultancy fees were purportedly bankrolled by the Kuwaiti government, which was keen to be protected from possible Iraqi incursions into its oil reserves and wealth. Kuwait basically wanted the United States involved as its bodyguard.

Part of H&K's PR arsenal was a testimony from a 15-year-old female Kuwaiti hospital worker whose full identity had to be kept confidential lest reprisals were made against her family. Known only as 'Nayirah', the girl shocked American Congress and TV audiences worldwide with tales of how she saw invading Iraqi troops throw babies from incubators onto hospital floors, where they were left to die. This highly emotive revelation moved many people and shifted public opinion towards the backing of a war.

However, the girl was actually a member of the Kuwaiti Royal Family. Her father, Saud Nasir al-Sabah, was Kuwait's Ambassador to the United States. More than that, rumours surfaced that Hill & Knowlton's vice-president Lauri Fitz-Pegado had personally coached 'Nayirah' on how to best deliver her false testimony. Nayirah's 'performance' was a key inclusion in a suite of media-ready materials prepared by a pressure group called 'Citizens for a Free Kuwait', effectively a PR-managed front for the pro-war camp.

Although highly influential at the time, Nayirah's tearful tale was later shown to be a complete lie; a fabrication engineered by PR people.

Accounted for

Subsequent attempts to verify Nayirah's testimony failed. Even Amnesty International which, along with most of the world's media, had become vocal after the incubator tale, was forced to issue an embarrassing retraction. Latterly, an attempt by the Canadian Broadcasting Corporation to interview Nayirah to clarify the circumstances surrounding the incident was angrily dismissed by her father Nasir al-Sabah. Nasir was able to use diplomatic privilege to rebuff any attempts to force him or his family to speak about the matter.

LESSONS LEARNT

They say that truth is often the first casualty of war and from this sorry episode we could add that ethics, integrity, honesty and respect for people's intelligence were also caught in the exchanges outlined. Of course, when one of the PR profession's core pledges to 'conduct ourselves professionally, with truth, accuracy, fairness and responsibility to the public' seems to have been violated by any of the discipline's highest-profile exponents, one is left to ponder the true values and morals of the PR 'profession' itself.

Publicity – Falling fowl of public opinion

Media spin:
'Asylum seekers plight used to peddle chickens'

The Age

South African-owned fast food retailer Nando's launched a radio advertising campaign in Australia that poked fun at illegal immigrant detainees. At the time, the issue of asylum seekers being kept in detention centres was a very contentious and high-profile one, which stirred strong emotions in the 'lucky country'.

Nando's launched its campaign hoping that the move would cause controversy and so net it widespread publicity that would exceed its relatively modest advertising spend.

Communications offensive

In its campaign, the roast chicken restaurant chain suggested that protesting detainees who had painfully sewn their lips together – in protest at having no say while being held in Australia's various detention centres – would find Nando's latest food offer irresistible. In a mock, news-anchorman voice-over, the advert claimed that detainees: 'decided to unsew their lips after hearing the news that with every

Nando's chicken combo, Nando's are giving away an extra chicken quarter free'.

Tasteless doesn't quite encapsulate this tacky creative tack. Even after being roundly condemned by the media, sections of the public and certainly the majority of the advertising industry's luminaries, Nando's continued to run its communications offensive.

The Advertising Federation of Australia chastised Nando's, saying that the campaign breached the industry's voluntary code of ethics and reminding the chicken fryers that: '[advertising] needs to gauge the temperature of consumers about sensitive issues. To use the refugee issue is appalling and is nothing more than a cheap shot'. Editorials and readers' letters condemning the campaign appeared in several Australian newspapers and also on ABC radio.

Nando's freely admitted that the campaign, which included print and in-store advertisements, was deliberately designed to attract media attention. However, the firm tried to emulate a Benneton-style defence by suggesting that the company really wanted to 'challenge the public to debate the issue'.

Or was the company just looking for loads of free publicity – for chicken feed – by any means that it could? It certainly seemed that empathetic and responsive PR was off the menu down at Nando's.

LESSONS LEARNT

In Public Relations practice, the concept of 'right conduct' demands that campaigns and strategies are executed in ways that are appropriate to the moral values held to be the norm in any given society. While this campaign's theme and execution may have been too hard to swallow for most fair-minded Aussies, Nando's was nonetheless able to report an upsurge in business as a result of the 'sewn lips' campaign. It begs the question: was the campaign almost perversely in tune with a silent majority Down Under?

Public opinion – The offal truth

Media spin:

'Gummer enlists daughter in BSE fight'

BBC News

The popularity of media photocalls can be understood when we consider the adage that 'a picture paints a thousand words'. Photocalls offer the chance for organizations to 'show' – a more potent way of communicating information – as well as to simply 'tell'. This may have been the prime motivation when one of the most tasteless and, retrospectively, perilous PR photocalls ever was staged by the then British government's minister for agriculture, John Gummer, in 1990.

At the height of the BSE – or Mad Cow disease – epidemic, the British government was under pressure on a number of fronts: the public was fearful that strains of BSE could leap species; the fast food industry was fearful that scares over infected beef could decimate its livelihood; farmers were facing the reality of seeing their stock devalued (literally and metaphorically) and many interests within the UK – principally local governments – were restricting and even banning the use of beef in places under their jurisdiction. Overseas, several of Britain's European neighbours were increasingly moving towards bans on British beef.

Despite fears emanating from a number of sources the Conservative government had effectively kept a lid on the BSE affair, taking the line that the risk of inter-species transfer was 'remote'.

Cat among the pigeons

This strategy had been working well until news broke of a cat – ironically called Max – that had died from a 'mad cow'-like infection. 'Mad Max' catapulted the issue back onto the top of the media agenda, with the government forced into a series of qualifications, clarifications and obfuscations designed to ensure that there was no widespread public panic.

To allay fears and demonstrate his personal confidence in the safety of British beef, Agriculture Minister Gummer pulled a publicity stunt where he fed his four-year-old daughter, Cordelia, with a Blighty beefburger in front of TV cameras and press photographers. Although intended to portray assurance of British beef's safety – there was no way a loving father would give his child poisoned food – Cordelia shied away from the burger. The stunt looked stilted and staged, and Gummer's little girl appeared uncomfortable and somewhat put-upon.

Gummer was panned for the callousness of the way he had been prepared to gamble with his own child's health; rumours abounded of cases where people had become gravely ill after eating contaminated beefburgers. If Gummer was prepared to take those kinds of risks with his own offspring, people read, what chance was there that he'd have genuine concerns for people he didn't know at all?

PR efforts beefed up

New to his ministerial position, Gummer may simply have been trying to improve upon the poor PR practised by his predecessor, Douglas Hogg, who had little or no media rapport. And in Gummer's defence, specialist government advisers had ruled out links between BSE and CJD, the human version of the disease that had parallel symptoms.

In a little-reported fact, Gummer later told an independent enquiry into the BSE affair that he'd been challenged by a newspaper to show his belief in beef by feeding it to his daughter. If Gummer's claim was true, the stunt that has gone down in media history as one of the most unsavoury ever devised was actually engineered by newspapermen!

Ultimately, though, Gummer made the decision to go along with it.

LESSONS LEARNT

When dealing with space- and time-pressed media, the photocall can enhance comprehension of the message needing to be relayed, with the visual dynamic also improving the likelihood of media coverage.

But for photocalls to successfully capture media attention – their very *raison d'être* – they either have to be theatrically contrived or in some way surprising. What was surprising was that a government minister would deploy his own child in a propaganda offensive, where the media and public suspected that they were getting a false and one-sided version of the BSE story.

Moreover, a couple of things had been ill-judged in Gummer's beefburger photocall, and contributed to the perceptions of a 'spin'. While kids love fast food, they love it when they love it, not necessarily when they are told to. Also, kids don't like to have dozens of pairs of eyes feasting on them as they feast on their burger; it makes them feel shy. Both factors kicked into play when Gummer passed the patty to his daughter.

The impression given was that a defenceless child was being force-fed potentially dangerous food and used as a pawn in a piece of manipulative government propaganda. But just as a child doesn't appreciate being force-fed, neither does the public.

Q

Quotes

Quotes

The predisposition of some individuals to 'sound off' before thinking of possible consequences has caused many a sleepless night for PR personnel called upon to handle the aftermath of careless quotes and quips.

This chapter features some of the higher-profile examples of when unscripted utterances make the job of the PR person utterly impossible.

Bar humbug

Royal Bank of Scotland Deputy Chairman Sir George Mathewson was in no mood to toast his latest corporate bonus. Despite receiving £750,000 as his share of a £2.5 million package awarded to a small cohort of bank directors, Sir George dismissed the award, saying that it 'wouldn't have given you bragging power in a Soho wine bar'.

So piffling did he think the amount, in fact, that neither he nor his fellow awardees had bothered to seek shareholder approval for it. Not surprisingly, the money and the arrogance angered many of the bank's shareholders who aired their gripes through a variety of media organs. Mathewson's 'bragging rights' comments featured centrally in a clutch of stories that scrutinized fat cats, executive perks, corporate governance as well as that hoary old chestnut, the banking sector's indifference to customers.

A credit to his bank

Barclays Chief Executive Matthew Barrett was scorned and ridiculed when the media reported how he said he never used his bank's credit card because it was too expensive.

Never mind that the bank's major domo didn't quite say that, actually making the point that he didn't like to pile up debt on a credit card because it (the practice of accumulating debt on credit) was too expensive. At the time, Barrett was responding in court – and under oath – to a select committee quizzing him on why his firm's subsidiary, Barclaycard, had an interest rate of almost 18 per cent at a time when rates had been falling and when the Bank of England's figure was a comparatively low 3.5 per cent.

It could have been reported that Barrett was speaking truthfully and actually advocating the responsible use of credit cards. After all, don't the media want frankness and truth from corporations? But Barrett gave newshounds another pearl by seemingly volunteering that he actively discouraged his four children from using credit cards altogether. Again, what he actually said, when you read between the editorial fine lines, was: 'I give them advice not to pile up debts on their credit cards.'

That's different to telling them not to use them at all, though, isn't it? Still, the media compared Barrett's candour to the gaffe made by former trinket magnate Gerald Ratner, he of the 'our products are crap' infamy, and so the image of Barclays and of the chief exec himself took a rather hefty knock.

Marks out of 10

Private company Camelot, administrator of Britain's National Lottery, was faced with an embarrassing PR gaffe after its Chief Executive Dianne Thompson told an audience of rapt marketers (plus one or two rat snitches) that lottery punters 'would be lucky to win a tenner'.

When a pip-squeak informed the media, Camelot was forced onto the offensive, nimbly deflecting attention by announcing that a new game – coincidentally with thousands of £10 prize-winning tickets – would be launched the following month.

She ain't just whistlin' Dixie

Natalie Maines, lead singer of all-woman country band Dixie Chicks, provoked a chorus of disapproval and created a PR crisis for her group when she flagged her opposition to the second war in Iraq.

Playing an overseas concert in London, Natalie quipped to a largely anti-war British audience that she was ashamed that President George Dubya also came from her home state of Texas. Retaliatory attacks were swift and largely merciless; incensed by Maines' moans, Dixie Chicks fans stateside publicly trashed and stomped on the band's CDs and posters while hollerin' for a national boycott of the traitorous trio. The irate fans' protests made for great media fodder, fuelling extensive news reports and national debates on patriotism and treachery, with largely negative press coverage dedicated to Maines' pronouncement.

Sales of the perceived peaceniks' latest CD release bombed as the Chicks got a hickory roasting from country music fans and press, particularly in the USA's southern states where national patriotism means unquestioning loyalty to government decisions about going to war. Vitriol against the band continued with the further burning of concert tickets and T-shirts and even vandalism of a band member's home, causing the trio to beef up their personal security. Patently, the backlash against Maines' political stance had taken the girls by surprise – or had it?

A rearguard rallying campaign saw the Chicks appear on national TV, to humbly assert that they supported the US troops but not the war they were fighting in. Then, with a whole lot less humility and modesty, they appeared naked on the cover of *Entertainment Weekly* their skin daubed with slogans such as 'Dixie Sluts', 'Saddam's Angels' and also the words 'Brave' and 'Hero'. In this, the girls had put their best foot – and other attractive body bits – forward in a provocatively controversial way. Everybody in the United States knew of the Dixie Chicks by then. If controversy doesn't actually sell, then it at least promotes awareness of a band and its products to audiences all over the land.

So was the initial quip calculating? I believe not. But was the PR fightback both creative and completely opportunistic? You betcha.

Tears of a clown

When Canadian Geoffrey Giuliano hung his head and shamefully announced his regret at how he'd made a living, executives at fast food chain McDonald's groaned as another PR disaster in the making was served up.

Geoffrey, one actor out of an estimated 250 who, at any given time, make a comfortable living playing the Ronald McDonald clown, parted company with McDonald's who were concerned that he was not fully walking the corporate talk. Geoffrey peeled off his carroty red wig, offering the following tasty titbits as his parting words to any interested media: 'I brainwashed youngsters into doing wrong,' plus the damning: 'I was the happy face on something that was horrendous.'

Of course, the ultimate insult for the other burger king was delivered when Geoffrey revealed his biggest secret: he had been a closet vegetarian for nearly 10 years. Deciding that the chips didn't need to stay down, however, Geoffrey followed the lead set by a former Marlboro man and began a counter-campaign designed to bite the hand that had previously fed him.

Mad dogs and Englishmen

For any director of a high-profile public company, being filmed partaking of the hospitality offered in a Spanish brothel is rarely considered as personally or professionally image-enhancing. And to be caught on tape deriding staff and customers alike, well, there's simply no way back from that, is there?

Freddy Shepherd and Doug Hall, directors of English football team Newcastle United, were caught doing all of the above in a *News Of The World* 'sting'. The covert operation heard the men derogatorily refer to the club captain Alan Shearer as Mary Poppins, ridiculing former manager Kevin Keegan and laughing at loyal supporters who pay large sums for the club's replica sports kit. Further, they denounced women from the Newcastle area as 'dogs'.

The extensive flak generated by the revelations – published in a national newspaper – put pressure on Shepherd and Hall to resign, which they did. But remarkably, when the fur had stopped flying, the two were re-employed by the club, which only goes to show how football really is a funny old game.

Media training

In the aftermath of London's Paddington train crash in October 1999, which saw four people die and many more seriously injured, Railtrack Chief Executive, Gerald Corbett, derailed his firm's reputation with a few ill-chosen words.

While trying to express some doubtless genuine sadness to the media and some of the grief-stricken relatives of those killed in the crash, he contrived to express how the pursuit of rail safety was 'a journey which has no end'. The unfortunate lexical choice was too much to bear for the more emotional of the attendees whose recently departed loved ones had been on a train journey that fatally had no end. The comments opened up the floodgates for welled-up tears plus a tide of media criticism for Corbett's accidental gaffe.

Having learnt nothing from his boss's PR blunder, another Railtrack director, Richard Middleton, gave a national radio interview in which he insisted that: 'It really is time for the hysteria around rail safety to be calmed down.' Grieving relatives may have been too suffused with their own personal hysteria to counter Middleton's remark, but a clutch of opinion formers, including the government's Deputy Prime Minister John Prescott weren't. Middleton subsequently apologized for any additional upset that his comments caused.

No smoke without fire

Charles Harper, Chairman of tobacco giants RJ Reynolds, unguardedly commented at an AGM meeting that he couldn't understand the furore surrounding children and passive smoking. Surely if the children don't like being in a smoky environment, they can simply leave it, he asserted. However, he saved his most enlightened pronouncement for last.

When further pressed as to how his view was applicable to infants, Harper simply opined – doubtless sending Reynolds' PR team into apoplexy – that at some point they'll learn to crawl.

Colourful language

Watching England's sole surviving representatives, Chelsea, struggling to get a good result against high-flying French side, Monaco, in the Champion's League competition, had clearly taken its toll on football commentator Ron 'Big Ron' Atkinson.

Distressed by the London team's 3–1 loss, Ron had completed his expert analysis commentary at Monaco's home ground and was watching re-runs of the game's key incidents, some featuring mistakes that had led to the Chelsea defeat.

Excluded from a live studio discussion being broadcast from his employer's London studios, Atkinson felt free to vent the frustrations that he had experienced while watching Chelsea's capitulation. Unbeknown to him, however, his studio microphone was still on.

Picking up on all of Atkinson's expletives, Big Ron's comments were broadcast via a live feed to a programme in the Middle East, where audiences there heard the hitherto respected Atkinson chastise Chelsea's captain and black defender Marcel Desailly with the words, 'He's what's known in some schools as a f***ing lazy thick nigger'.

On realizing that his comments had gone to air, Atkinson tendered his resignation, which was immediately accepted by ITV bosses. The loss of one of Ron's 'nice little earners' was swiftly followed by another: London broadsheet *The Guardian* cancelled a weekly column Atkinson had been writing for its sports pages.

Then the soft drink company 7Up, which was using 'Big Ron' as the figurehead of a quest to find football's funniest quote, also ripped up its contract with the football pundit. Atkinson was fast finding himself alone in the media wilderness.

Admitting his culpability, Atkinson did the honourable thing and put his hands up for the error. He appeared on national TV news to admit that he had made a bad mistake, but to deny that he was racist. However, Ron's 'I know it's a racist statement, but I didn't intend it to be a racist statement...' offered little defence or excuse for the use of a four-word phrase comprising three abhorrent insults and an accentuating adjective.

Clothes maketh the man

When the brand director of one of the UK's leading men's fashion chain stores gave an interview with a retail trade magazine, he said that its customers were 'hooligans'.

By way of explanation, Top Man's David Shepherd explained that Top Man customers only wore suits on two occasions: for their first job interview and for a court appearance. Of course, David's remarks were picked up and commented on by many UK dailies, causing hooligan-like howls of protests at many of the company's stores. Very fitting.

Joke over shark finishes career

The skilful orator will readily regale you with the advantages of being able to incorporate humour into a speech or presentation. Striking just the right note of levity – usually with a judicious and light touch – can help you make the 'emotional' connection with your audience, which helps them to warm to you.

Another key for the successful delivery of a comedic comment is that the remark should be contemporary, yet the deft touch completely deserted a British Tory party MP who made a bad taste joke regarding the recent death of 20 suspected Chinese immigrants.

The mass death had occurred when 19 people drowned after being swept away by powerful tides as they collected cockles in Morecambe Bay off the north east coast of England. Another body – possibly the 20th victim – was found a week and a half later.

Speaking at a dinner for a mixed crowd of English and Danish businessmen not long after the tragedy, Tory MP Anne Winterton addressed the ensemble with a joke about two sharks that were sick of eating tuna. In her tale, one of the sharks quipped 'So, let's go to Morecambe for a Chinese'.

Lambasted for the tasteless joke by her Tory party peers, Winterton refused to apologize or retract the comments, casting her Conservative colleagues in a particularly unflattering light, because Winterton's words were decidedly bad for party PR. Conservative leader Michael Howard announced her effective dismissal from the party, citing her failure to recant the unacceptable comments which, he said, 'have no place in the Conservative Party'.

The incident shows the real cost of using a cheap joke when making a public address. Certain jokes can cause embarrassment if broadcast to a wider audience. It's essential that if you're tempted to use humour, it should always be appropriate to the situation and to your position or role at that time. If not, it might come back to bite you.

LESSONS LEARNT

As the move towards reality-style TV shows suggests, the incursion of the media into every nook and cranny of public and private life is increasing. What this means for PR personnel charged with preservation of reputation, is that every comment – corporate or casual, official or off-the-cuff – made by representatives of any company or organization is subject to media, and therefore public, scrutiny. From a PR management viewpoint, there's a pressing requirement to brief company representatives about their oratory responsibilities, and to educate them as to the potential consequences of careless quips.

Regular media training, for example, develops skills that can preclude verbal disasters. This training fosters the understanding that public-facing staff are always, effectively, on company business irrespective of their situation or location. They must be made aware that the media makes no distinction between public and private life and makes fewer allowances for personal arrogance and prejudices, emotional outbursts or even genuine linguistic lapses.

Company spokespeople need to learn the power of 'pausing before pronouncing', which affords them the time to consider the likely impact of their words. Executive officers, for example, must appreciate that a comment that makes them seem witty and urbane among their peers, may seem wicked and unwarranted to a different stakeholder group. This mini 'waiting game' should also encourage them to assess their motivation or the desired effect when giving a quote. Management staff must remember that their principal job is not to entertain, but to best represent the organization that employs them.

Of course, unwise words are occasionally used to deliberately damage a company's reputation by departing employees or, occasionally, by mischievous media. Good issues and crisis management plans are essential if any PR disaster fires are to be effectively doused.

It's a working reality, too, that company representatives can sometimes be quoted out of context, so causing PR discomfort. PR practitioners are quite at liberty to ask media for a retraction or correction, but their time would be better spent discreetly informing their key stakeholders most affected of the truth of the matter.

Finally, is it recommended to use a contentious quote to catalyse a double-edged media furore that creates screeds of editorial coverage that optimizes public exposure, as in the case of the Dixie Chicks? To me, that was one lucky PR victory skilfully rescued from the fast-closing jaws of defeat, and not a course of action recommended for those for whom PR job security is paramount.

Radio,
Reputation Management,
Research,
Rumour Management

Radio – Promotion leaves station cooling its heels

Media spin:
'Radio station guilty over frozen buttocks'
Yahoo News

In the world of promotions, it seems there's no such thing as a new idea, so it's perhaps inevitable that, in the quest for innovation, some of the fresher creative tacks could be construed as being more than a little 'out there'. And where there's creative wackiness involved, there's plenty of scope for disastrous PR.

The PR bods at English radio station BRMB decided on an innovative competition for listeners to win tickets and VIP prizes for a live music extravaganza called 'Party in the Park'. As the competition was designed for fans to win the 'coolest seats in town', the challenge went out for four listeners who could endure sitting on blocks of ice.

Conceptually it's a nice idea with strong 'linkage' (as we say in PR parlance) between cool seats and blocks of ice. And it was probably pretty cheap to do as well. Physiologically, though, it was bad. Very bad. Sitting on ice for too long (even if it's covered with plastic sheeting) causes burns. On the day of the event, the BRMB contestants were rushed to the local Sellyoaks Hospital, one with 18 per cent burns to the legs and thighs and another suffering painfully damaged buttocks.

Covering its own backside

Although the station hadn't covered the contestants' backsides properly, it thought it had covered its own. For they'd been prescient enough to pass the stunt through legals before the competition started. This established the failsafe that all entrants had to sign disclaimers before participating and precluded any of the pained participants from being able to personally sue the station for the discomfort caused. However, a court case was pursued and BRMB was eventually fined £15,000 and had to issue a humiliating public apology to those injured. And saying sorry rarely looks cool.

LESSONS LEARNT

For a hip and edgy radio station to demonstrate its maverick nature by encouraging its listeners to go to extremes to win gig tickets might be considered acceptable. It can certainly make for good 'on air' content. But when going to those extremes damages its listeners' extremities then the prank has obviously gone too far. Failure to think through the consequences of this promotional stunt, no matter how sexy the headline 'Coolest seats in town' appeared, merely shows evidence of half-assed PR thinking.

Putting publicity before the safety of the target audience is never excusable, especially when the potential negative publicity leaves a decided chill in relations between the station and its offended audience.

Reputation management – Even playing field

Media spin:

'200,000 more Games tickets for the rich'

Sydney Morning Herald

The 2000 Sydney Olympics was hyped as being the best Games the world would ever see: the world's greatest sporting spectacle hosted by the world's most sport-loving nation.

With the predicted influx of foreign visitors, the event organizers, the Sydney Organizing Committee for the Olympic Games (SOCOG), still needed to ensure that the event was well supported by Australians, too. So, an extensive advertising and marketing communications campaign promised ticket allocation would be organized by a totally fair and open public ballot, which would give every Australian an equal chance to get a seat at the Olympics – even a seat at some of the most coveted events.

Taken at face value

SOCOG's comprehensive marketing plan worked a treat, with Australians spending close to AU $350 million in advance for Olympic Games tickets. However, the press got wind that SOCOG had secretly removed thousands of 'best seat' tickets and assigned them to an exclusive premium ticket scheme for individuals and companies prepared to pay a premium price of up to three times the tickets' original face value. This meant that the majority of the best tickets were not available as promised in SOCOG's initial promotions for the Games.

It transpired that the general public, via ballot applications, had only a 2 per cent chance of getting seats for top events. Most of those who got tickets via the ballot had to be content with their second or third choice event.

Seat of power

Other allegations followed, with some SOCOG board members accused of cronyism – ie helping friends and associates to get back door access to the 'best seats'. These allegations got a very public airing in the Australian media, which likes nothing better than to chop down 'tall poppies'. And when the media stink wouldn't go away, the great and the good of SOCOG got downright bad and ugly, informing on their colleagues and trying to distance themselves from any impropriety.

This was exemplified when SOCOG President and Olympics Minister, Michael Knight and Chief Executive Sandy Holloway denied all knowledge of the premium price ticket scheme. This signalled bad news for Paul Reading, the executive who had supposedly devised the scam to make up a budget deficit.

First, Reading's position was downgraded and then he departed from the organization with confusion surrounding whether he had jumped or was pushed. Again, this confusion was extensively covered in the Australian media.

Competition intensifies

The brouhaha that this episode stirred up also stimulated the interest of the nation's corporate watchdog the ACCC (Australian Competition and Consumer Commission). Its investigation concluded by accusing SOCOG of deceptive and misleading conduct, which is a serious offence under consumer protection law. Consequently, under extreme pressure SOCOG was forced to offer refunds to the people who did not get their first choice tickets and it also undertook to take seats out of the premium scheme and put them back into the second round ballot. Naturally, the media interest in these developments was as strong as it had been with all the prior revelations.

Game plan

As this crisis unfolded, one might have expected some humility or regret from SOCOG but neither was forthcoming, which further outraged the media and public alike. In fact, when the ticketing irregularities came to light, SOCOG's response was actually one of dismissive arrogance. Not only did this PR disaster mean that PR staff became embroiled in dousing media fires, but it limited the time they had to spend on communicating the many positive aspects of the world's greatest sporting spectacle.

LESSONS LEARNT

The actions of the SOCOG board bore several hallmarks of how not to handle a crisis of significant public interest.

Management of an issue that clearly revealed that SOCOG had acted improperly and misled the public looked, to most outsiders, bungled. First, they stonewalled, which gave the impression that they had something to hide and that they were impervious to the concerns being expressed by their stakeholders. Then they hesitated when they should have taken positive, remedial action, which would have lessened the vitriolic attacks that soon came their way. Failure to resolve the matter quickly and satisfactorily only served to keep the issue alive, drawing in other organizations such as the ACCC, which dragged SOCOG into litigation. Taking any issue into the law courts means that the dirty laundry gets washed and aired in full view of the public.

Throughout, there was also a lack of strong leadership from SOCOG; strong in this context doesn't mean fighting strong or unflinching strong: it should mean someone responsible enough to accept and deal with the consequences of wrongdoing. And the frantic attempts at personal skin-saving did little to diffuse suspicions of malpractice. This – and the 'scapegoating' of Paul Reading – also raised public ire in a country where 'mateship' is held in high regard.

In a case of obvious wrongdoing, an organization really only has one option, which is to come clean and tell the full story. Failure to do so means that you are taken further away from quickly capping a troublesome situation, which can result in tortuously drawn out, negative publicity.

In business as in sport, it all comes down to playing fair.

Research – Own goal for football brand

Media spin:
'Umbro "regrets" Holocaust blunder'
www.cnn.com

While PR theorists and academics place great stock in the role of research in the communication process, PR commonly gets involved as the one following the parade with the shovels when other communications disciplines are less than diligent with their research. Like when sports goods and apparel manufacturer Umbro named one of its children's ranges of training shoes 'Zyklon', thereby provoking outrage from an influential Jewish rights group.

Political football

Documenting its concerns, the Simon Weisenthal Centre lambasted the name 'Zyklon' as 'an encouragement to neo-Nazis who terrorize the football terraces and a dishonour to sport itself'. The Centre's Dr Shimon Samuels reminded Umbro that 'Zyklon' was the name given to a deadly nerve gas used by Nazi Germany in the Second World War death camps. Dr Samuels implicitly condemned Umbro for its commercial use of a word strongly associated with mass murder.

Umbro expressed regret for any offence caused and suggested that an internal investigation into what could only have been an accident would be undertaken. This partly addressed the Simon Weisenthal Centre's demand for an 'investigation and condemnation of those behind Umbro's marketing strategy'. At the same time, Umbro pointed out that the offending 'Zyklon' name had only been used in ads and not on the training shoes themselves. This attempt to bring some perspective may have looked somewhat lame given that more people probably read adverts than read words on a shoe.

Yet true to prescribed crisis management diffusion techniques, Umbro underlined that it had already changed the name of the shoe in the UK with plans to follow up that remedial action internationally.

LESSONS LEARNT

As the concept of branding is all about image, it's easy to see how there should be a role for PR in the process of developing and growing brands. PR skills are valuable in helping to predict the consequences of the new brand's emergence among stakeholder groups and not just market segments. In other words, while marketing and advertising are largely focused on sales, Public Relations is focused on a bigger picture and so, a wider audience. It's amazing to think that in the development of a mass-market sports shoe sub-brand, no-one asked the question, 'What does the name mean?' Perhaps Public Relations could have dug around to find this out, thereby reaffirming its value to the brand development process. In this episode, Umbro effectively handled the situation, empathizing with concerns and confirming that action was being taken to correct any perceived wrongdoing. It's a simple but reliable way to get a positive result in the world of reputation management.

Rumour management – Devil of a stain mars reputation

Rumours are possibly the most damaging and difficult to dispel of all influences on organizational reputation. In the mid-1970s, Procter & Gamble became associated with allegations suggesting that it was a 'front organization' for Satanism. This rumour was thought to have been around since the company was formed in the late 1800s. If true, the corporation was unbelievably lax in preparing its rumour management strategy!

No-go logo

Mischievous 'bizlore' suggested that P&G's original owners had traded Satan's promise of success in exchange for permission to represent his logo on all their products: an early form of sponsorship, if you like.

Some speculated that the reason the rumours started to resurface around 1974 was that P&G decided to revert to the use of its original logo showing a bearded 'man in the moon' looking over 13 stars, representing each of the original 13 US colonies. Gossip and hearsay insisted that the number 666 – supposedly the mark of the devil – was discernible on the wispy threads of the old man's beard.

Unchristian behaviour

Suspecting that a competitive business interest – specifically Amway – was engaged in perpetuating the rumours, Proctor & Gamble feared a backlash against its products, particularly among Christian communities in the United States and mainland Europe. As Amway is a direct sales organization, many of its staff had developed personal relationships with thousands of customers. This could have enabled them to use 'word of mouth' – the most potent and influential form of communication – to spread the gossip. Before long, however, P&G acquired taped evidence that Amway staff had actively spread the Satanic slurs.

Quash the goss

In its defence, Amway admitted that some remarks had been made by one of its people, but insisted it had instructed the staffer to make a retraction before the employee and the company parted ways. Amway's defence lawyer actually blamed Procter & Gamble's 'botched PR' as being mostly to blame for the widespread interest in the rumours, although P&G had conducted a comprehensive counter-information campaign via freecall phone lines, extensive journalist briefings and media relations activities, as well as stakeholder communications delivered from church pulpits!

But yet again, media reportage of the legal proceedings didn't exactly help to quash the goss. Word had really caught on and P&G was feeling the pinch.

The calling

Such was the widespread interest in the devilish rumours that Procter & Gamble's customer relations team was thought to be handling around 15,000 calls every month from people looking for information about the firm's satanic connections. Needless to say, the firm's PR team was kept very busy countering the allegations and contending with new evolutions of the rumours, which surfaced again some 20 years later.

Show and tell

In 1995 an anonymous flyer and e-mail claimed that the president of Procter & Gamble had appeared on a national talk show, 'Donahue', in the USA confirming that his firm had demonic links and that company profits were channelled in support of a satanic church.

Despite proving that these claims were entirely bogus and that the TV segment was a complete fabrication (although the 'Donahue' show certainly exists) the P&G brand's Achilles heel was again exposed. This time, the rumours were so persistent that they forced P&G into a logo redesign, with the company opting to create two new and more corporate-looking logos, which featured a script typeface in place of the old man with the beard. And while the company decided not to bin the old logo entirely – it was retained as the company's official trademark – a design facelift saw the removal of the wispy beard that was rumoured to include the devilish number 666.

Obviously the cost to P&G for such an exercise was massive – replacing a multinational logo on everything from stationery to vehicle livery and product packaging doesn't come cheap. There was similarly high expenditure on the PR effort associated with continually playing down slurs that seemed deliberately engineered and propagated to cause consumers to stop buying P&G products.

LESSONS LEARNT

Due to their ethereal nature, gossip and urban myths can be impossible to identify and intercept, creating major tracking problems. The difficulty for the PR consultant in a rumour management scenario is how to fight an enemy that you cannot see, hear or pin down, especially when their next appearance can be highly difficult to predict. Depending on the severity of the rumour, organizations may just have to accept the challenge of continually countering debilitating negative media coverage that can have a detrimental impact on business. This may involve establishing a rumour hotline, utilizing a credible, independent rumour refuter, acting responsibly to re-establish trust, conducting regular and open stakeholder communications and trying to prepare for, or proactively head off, new outbreaks.

If all this fails, one might consider taking quicker than 90 years to kill off an anecdotal rumour that forces an eventual redesign of a global logo, the symbolism of which was vulnerable to speculative interpretation.

S

Smear Campaigns,
Soundbites,
Speeches,
Spokespeople,
Sports PR,
Stakeholder Relations,
Stunts

Smear campaigns – Virgin sullied but reputation intact

Media spin:
'Bitter taste of airline feud'
BBC Online

There's no doubt that, as the eyes and ears of many businesses, the Public Relations function can be highly effective at identifying those forces that could potentially impact on the organization. And, as a representative voice, PR can be equally useful in influencing public perceptions. With its great awareness of all potential influences and the ability to develop relationships with them, PR is ideally placed to help shape corporate image.

However, when PR is deployed to negatively influence the brand image of competitive interests, there's ample potential for the misuse of weaponry in the PR arsenal. Two PR consultants representing airline giant British Airways saw their professionalism and standing go into a talespin after they were implicated in the execution of a strategy specifically designed to undermine confidence in a new market entrant.

Airspace invaders

When fledgling aviation company Virgin – with a start-out fleet of just six aeroplanes – tried to establish a presence within the British airline industry in the late 1980s, the sector's dominant player, British Airways, seemed hell-bent on rebuffing any incursion into its airspace.

Virgin's maverick boss, Richard Branson – a savvy and successful entrepreneur – reckoned that the squeeze being put on his business was not only constricting, but also illegal. With an intuitive feel and renown for utilizing the power of media relations, Branson publicly challenged what he claimed were BA's unfair business practices. Taking his message to the media in early 1991, Branson cited BA's illegal practice of swamping the market with low-cost fares which, although making a loss for BA, effectively discouraged airline passengers from choosing Virgin seats on similar transatlantic routes.

BA dismissively refuted Virgin's allegations with a public utterance that would, ironically, come back to bite the market-leader at a later date. 'Mr Branson would do better to run his own business efficiently rather than attack the competition,' was its pronouncement.

Aerial attacks

However, rumours persisted that BA was itself engaged in attacks on the Virgin business model. Whispers claimed that BA had hacked into confidential passenger booking systems to find out the names and contact numbers of passengers who had booked with Virgin.

It later emerged that some of these passengers had been cold-called at home and offered free tickets, upgrades and bonus air miles if they'd revert to BA. Some passengers were even 'button-holed' and given the hard sell near the Virgin desks at Gatwick and JFK airports, where they were again offered compelling incentives to switch their allegiance back to BA.

Smarting from BA's aggressive customer retention strategies, Branson began legal proceedings against BA for remarks it had made in an official media release regarding Virgin's 'reliability record';

Branson felt that this statement was intended to mar his company's reputation.

Certainly BA had a tangible and very public disdain for Virgin that was evident in the tone of media communications emanating from BA's Public Affairs department. This crack unit was run by an Irish ex-militia man, David Burnside, then one of the UK's most influential and intimidating communications advisers.

Yet BA and its septuagenarian chairman, Lord King, were forced to take Virgin's presence a lot more seriously when the UK's Civil Aviation Authority initiated a move to liberalize traffic distribution at Britain's busiest airport, Heathrow, where BA had enjoyed years of unfettered dominance. When this move was ratified, Branson effected a cheeky piece of PR opportunism by posing for a media photocall at the entrance to Heathrow, dressed as a pirate.

Posing in front of a huge model of Concorde, the Virgin team had also cheekily covered the BA-owned Concorde's tailfin with a Virgin logo and surrounded the area with posters claiming Heathrow was now 'Virgin Territory'. PR one-upmanship and the media-friendly Branson's charisma ensured massive media coverage of the stunt and, more importantly, the fact that Virgin was seriously challenging BA's market dominance.

Dirty tricks

Its own 'Liberty-taking' Public Relations efforts aside, Virgin suspected that BA had been covertly executing a strategy designed to malign the new airline's reputation, with Branson declaring in the media that BA was running a 'dirty tricks' campaign. Virgin had got 'tale wind' that BA's Public Affairs team was behind a campaign to discredit Virgin with consumer and 'City' audiences.

Sources sympathetic to Branson confirmed that rumours – hinting at Shell's fictional unwillingness to supply fuel to Virgin because of credit control issues and suggesting that Virgin was dangerously under-resourced – had emanated from BA-related sources. The same sources had allegedly portrayed Branson as a dangerous eccentric, inferring that his business interests in a prominent London gay club somehow reflected the undesirability of his character.

Virgin suspected that London City PR supremo Brian Basham, an influential media consultant engaged by BA's PR chief David Burnside, was involved in the misleading and malicious information being leaked to business journalists.

BA's sowing of such scurrilous rumours could only have been intended to create a rift in relations between Virgin, its possible customers and the larger business community, potential investors included. But not averse to PR subterfuge itself, Virgin had a friendly journalist secretly tape some of the allegations being made to sully Virgin.

Board stiff

After unsuccessfully attempting to resolve the issues surrounding BA's business practices with the incumbent board, Branson presented his claims directly to BA's non-executive directors. His representations – mocked by BA management as self-serving attempts at publicity – again left the BA board completely unmoved.

By then, the media was intrigued by the public spat between the highly personable and unconventional Branson and Lord King, a shrewd but, compared to Branson, slightly dour establishment figure.

The combative approach BA had exhibited towards Virgin's attempted growth had not ameliorated and even when a TV documentary probed Branson's grievances and BA's practices, BA brazenly derided the claims, attributing them to Virgin's publicity drive.

Planely obvious

This was where PR's input really tripped matters up: BA published its rubbishing of Branson's claims in its in-house newsletter, *BA News*, and several external communiqués. The piece implied that because Branson's claims were unfounded, he must have been lying.

But because Branson had been acquiring proof of BA's anti-Virgin campaign, the article was libellous, so paving the way for Virgin to launch a court action against one of Britain's hitherto 'Teflon-coated' corporations. The panic this caused within the BA ranks was seismic; it culminated in a farcical scenario, which saw BA's PR chief Burnside meeting a supposed Virgin undercover agent in a Lancashire pub. Outside, BA's private detectives were trying to tape-record the rendezvous.

When news of this covert operation – codenamed 'Operation Covent Garden' – was leaked into the public domain, it brought not only the operation to a close, but also helped ground the high-flying corporate careers of Burnside, Basham and, eventually, Lord King himself.

Freefall

BA's own reputation went into freefall as it was brought to book by the judiciary, forced to pay court costs of around £4 million, as well as £610,000 in damages to Virgin and Branson. Nifty PR opportunism saw Branson distribute the award evenly among his own firm's staff, further galvanizing the support of his staunch internal stakeholders.

BA was alleged to have bled another £500,000 as part of a golden handshake given to its former PR chief, Burnside, who left the organization quickly and, more importantly, very quietly. BA legal representatives admitted the existence of the smear campaign and apologized unreservedly for its shameful conduct.

LESSONS LEARNT

As communications specialists are increasingly agreeing, PR is the key component in the creation of brand image; with a broader perspective than the other communications disciplines, PR is ideally positioned to astutely manage an entity's reputation. Remember that, essentially, brands are built on reputation.

The way that BA chose to meet Virgin's arrival in its marketplace – aggressively and at times illegally – reflected very badly on its own reputation and, consequently, on its own brand. The strategy adopted to protect its market seems, in hindsight, quite flawed. Most advertising gurus have long known the perils of adopting a 'knocking strategy' against competitive interests: it reflects badly on the company doing the knocking. The best way to demonstrate superiority is not to pinpoint the other party's alleged inferiority or dismiss it as a 'publicity-seeking' machine, but to promote your own strengths and attributes. Likewise, the aggression in BA's corporate rhetoric showed a pronounced yet completely unnecessary disdain for Branson and his airborne enterprise. BA's unwillingness to communicate with Virgin was seen as being arrogant and aloof.

Good business etiquette – and common sense PR advice – requires that a respectful, almost diplomatic restraint should be deployed when commenting on competitor activity; this approach can help take prejudicial emotion out of the representative tone of voice a business adopts.

As for PR's role in the tactical rollout of character assassinations, gossip-mongering, supplying false information, snooping on competitor operatives, being instrumental in corporate espionage and then being openly seen as the source of derogatory comments, both verbal and printed? The word 'unethical' probably sums it up best.

Perhaps BA's single greatest mistake was to underestimate the business nous and personable media charm of Branson. Few can play the game better than Richard.

BA's controversial anti-Virgin campaign is extensively documented in *Dirty Tricks*, a gripping expose of the air wars between BA and Virgin, written by Martyn Gregory.

Soundbites – When the chips are down

For those in the media spotlight, it's sometimes better to be thought a fool than to open your mouth and remove all doubt, as the old adage says.

The United States' ex-Vice President Dan Quayle, for one, knows only too well that politicians live and die by the soundbite. And the day that Dan told a sixth-grader that potato was spelt with an 'e' on the end, was the day that his political career got well and truly fried.

Republican Quayle was a man on a PR mission, pressing the flesh all over the United States to cultivate positive public opinion. Part of his hectic schedule involved attending a school drug education programme in Trenton, New Jersey, where he was to help officiate at a spelling bee, partly for the edification of the local media.

It seemed simple: read some words off a card and let the kids go up to the blackboard and write the correct spelling. But when 15-year-old William Figueroa spelt potato correctly and Dan the man offered his own alternative version, Quayle's career went into tailspin.

Roasting

A reporter from the local newspaper, *The Trentonian*, reported the incident to his editor who ran a front-page piece with exclusive quotes from Figueroa who professed to now understand why people thought Quayle 'an idiot'. National television picked up the story, giving Quayle a roasting for his gaffe, while the top-rating David Letterman invited Figueroa onto his show to share his experience. Figueroa tickled audiences by asking whether you had to go to college to become vice president.

Retrospectively, Quayle bemoaned the extent of the coverage and the personal jibes that followed what was, in essence, a pretty silly story involving a pretty silly human mistake. Yet starting with jokes about 'Mr Potato Head', the blunder played and played, eventually becoming a key weapon for the Democrats backing Gore and Clinton against the Republican Quayle and Bush.

Boiling

In the wake of Trenton, Quayle was said to be livid with his aides for putting him up for the spelling bee and with the media for making such a big deal about his gaffe. He was probably most upset at the embarrassment he'd brought upon himself, though. Quayle was said to be perpetually puzzled that his Democratic counterpart Al Gore's subsequent blooper that a leopard had changed its 'stripes' got nowhere near the amount of negative coverage that his potato blunder had.

In most political arenas of the Western world, image is everything, and Dan Quayle's personal image hadn't been too good to begin with. To many, he was a handsome 'smoothie', none too bright, who'd put his foot in it on more than one previous occasion. Considered a long way short of being an intellectual heavyweight, his spelling bee incident seemed to afford the media the opportunity to show how challenged his intellect really was.

LESSONS LEARNT

So, should Dan's communications advisers have put him up for the spelling bee? Could he perhaps have been given the cards to familiarize himself with the words and their spelling before the event started? On such a whistlestop PR tour, was there even time to do so? How do we know he might not have ad-libbed and made the same mistake, anyway? Even with the best preparations, communications advisers can never legislate for every possibility, such as when an educated man trips over the spelling of one word in a way that captures the attention of a nation's entire media system and influences public opinion on that man's suitability to hold public office.

Speeches – CEO caught pie-eyed

Media spin:
'Monsanto chief gets pie in the face'
The Global Citizen

Senior executives can take a leading role in communicating company philosophy and fostering productive public 'relationships' by making keynote speeches at seminars and lectures. With the CEO ostensibly exuding gravitas, the aims of such appearances can be to educate stakeholders, influence opinion-formers, galvanize support, or generate positive media coverage.

However, a trend has developed that has seen management executives put in the firing line as targets for 'soft protests' by factions opposed to their corporate viewpoint. 'Soft protests' typically include being assaulted with gooey and messy foodstuffs or daubed with coloured dyes. So it was that the Chief Executive of genetically engineered (GE) food producer, Monsanto, Robert Shapiro, found himself 'pie-eyed' and publicly embarrassed after being struck in the face with a tofu crème flan at a major 'State of the World Forum' in San Francisco.

Just desserts?

Having delivered his keynote address, Shapiro went to exit the stage, pausing briefly to respond to a heckler haranguing him from the crowd. With split-second precision, a unit of patisserie terrorists – thought to be an anti-genetics splinter faction of the Biotic Baking Brigade – capitalized on the stationary CEO, and splattered him with a creamy concoction.

The flan ambush – or 'flanbush' – sent shock waves through the predominantly corporate audience who'd paid $5,000 per ticket to dine and hear the bespectacled Shapiro talk up his company's role in saving the earth's dwindling natural resources. Instead, they'll have taken away the memory of him looking both dishevelled and decidedly rattled.

The ambushers' weapons, too, were carefully chosen: Shapiro copped a tofu crème pie, symbolically chosen to represent Monsanto's growing acres of so-called 'Frankenstein' soya bean crops. The other gustatory grenade was a sweet potato pie, specially baked to draw attention to Monsanto's new genetically engineered super-spud.

Yet the pastry pasting wasn't the only form of dissent on show at the forum; other activists had infiltrated the crowd before and during the event to disseminate copies of 'The Monsanto Files', a special edition of *The Ecologist* magazine, which asked searching questions of Monsanto's business practices.

Recipe for success

Although the pie perpetrators fled, they were soon captured by the venue's security and handed over to the San Francisco Police Department to face criminal charges. But this was no disaster to the activists, who fully appreciated how their arrest helped to increase the newsworthiness of the incident, thereby enhancing the likelihood that it would be reported upon: mission achieved!

There was a lot more method in this apparently madcap attack than might at first appear. 'Soft protests' involve a lot of planning and logistical nous. The activists sometimes stalk their targets for months and spend time gaining approved access to exclusive events. When an attack is imminent, 'flanners' usually dress in business suits to make themselves indistinguishable in the corporate throng.

LESSONS LEARNT

PR personnel are instrumental in creating opportunities for senior executives to walk the corporate talk. But as well as liaising with events organizers, preparing speeches and conducting pre- and post-event media relations, they need to become attuned to the potential publicity pitfalls and threats to security posed by the new breed of anti-corporate activists.

As those within this latter group have brought a new dynamic to the meaning of 'active publics', there are new dangers involved in public oration. As their agenda is diametrically opposed to that being proposed by corporates, activists have discovered that gentle aggression helps them to get noticed, without facing really harsh judicial penalties.

The activists' motivation in carrying out such public attacks is simple. By breaching security cordons and making their target look less than dignified in public, the stunt makes it onto the media agenda, prompting reporters to look into the circumstances surrounding the incidents, then reporting on them, so bringing any associated issues into the public domain. 'Flanning' offers a relatively cheap – and occasionally tasty – way of grabbing a share of media voice.

The reach of the 'flanbushers' is increasingly extensive. British MP Ann Widdecombe was splatted while signing copies of her novel at a bookstore in London. Ironically, the pieing probably attracted more publicity for the book's launch than Widdecombe's publishers could ever have hoped for. Even one of the world's richest and best-guarded men, Bill Gates, copped a face-full while addressing an audience.

All of this means that if PR people want to prevent the embarrassment of having public appearances turned into public humiliation, then designated 'executive security' needs to be added to the checklist for corporate public speaking engagements.

Spokespeople – Legal eagle sings the blues

Media spin:

'Findlay's song of hate'

Daily Record

It is well documented how sectarianism is a blight on football in Scotland's second city, Glasgow. Its two main clubs, Celtic and Rangers, principally draw support from the Roman Catholic and Protestant communities, respectively. The animosity between the teams' supporters partly mirrors the bigotry and 'troubles' of nearby Northern Ireland. Season to season, year on year, football-related violence is a feature of city life, forcing both clubs to speak out against sectarian intolerance.

Rangers' one-time vice chairman and sometime spokesperson, Donald Findlay, was one of Scotland's most eminent lawyers and an intelligent professional. All the more absurd, then, that Findlay should become embroiled in an incident that portrayed him and Rangers FC in a highly controversial light.

Music to their ears

The incident occurred when Findlay took a microphone at a Rangers' supporters club function and sang some fiercely Protestant songs including the notoriously provocative anthem, 'The Sash', much to the delight of his fellow revellers. Findlay's musical selection was virtually synonymous with the tribal partisan hatred of Northern Ireland. As he sang the anthems, he was flanked by a group of Rangers players that included at least two Catholics.

Unfortunately, his spirited rendition was captured on video camera and turned over to the Scottish media whose broadcast and publishing of the footage created a huge public outcry among more tolerant Scots. It was an unmitigated Public Relations disaster for Rangers FC which, at the time, was publicly professing to have dumped the baggage that came from having had a near century-old employment policy that forbade the signing of Roman Catholics.

Singing a different tune

On being 'outed' on video, Findlay immediately made the huge mistake of trying to claim that all three tunes were no more than 'historic folk songs'. He had forgotten the basic tenets of PR crisis management – truth, remorse and reparation. His failure to accept responsibility for the inappropriateness of his actions cut no ice with the media or the public, many of whom were painfully aware of the songs' divisive sentiments.

Findlay's feigned ignorance only encouraged pockets of the press to dig deeper into the broader issue of sectarianism in football and, specifically, Rangers' role in that. For Findlay, an acknowledged spokesperson for the club, to be filmed not just endorsing but celebrating bigotry through strong anti-Catholic sentiments left the club with no option. The club chairman, David Murray, accepted the lawyer's resignation. Murray had previously gone on record to insist that sport and sectarianism must be separated. Findlay was also reprimanded and fined for his antics by Scotland's Faculty of Advocates.

Whatever fuelled Findlay's actions torched all the previous efforts by Rangers to downplay its image as an anti-Catholic club. Moreover, his actions kicked back into touch an anti-bigotry alliance which both of the Glasgow football giants claimed to be united in tackling.

LESSONS LEARNT

Patently, Findlay failed to grasp how corporate image is a fluid concept that is as much determined by the behaviour and actions of those staff members in the public light as it is by logos and livery. In fact, good PR is often built on the integrity and ethics of a company's management and its public-facing personnel. Additionally, the 'public' makes no distinction between organizational life and private life. And in this situation, where personal, organizational, sporting and religious beliefs are unhealthily enmeshed, there was little leeway to make discerned distinctions and certainly not to excuse a club official's incendiary behaviour.

Sports PR – Kicked into touch

Media spin:
'Man Utd in Brazil – a waste of time?'
BBC News

When the world's most famous soccer team, Manchester United, visited the football-mad Brazilian capital of Rio de Janeiro to participate in a friendly tournament, there seemed limitless opportunities to secure acres of PR coverage.

Media training session

From the moment of touchdown at the airport in Rio, Manchester United and its band of fit and famous soccer celebrities received an enthusiastic welcome. It wasn't long, however, before United managed to metaphorically thumb their noses at their hosts by arranging a closed doors training session that excluded the media and locals alike, the club citing security concerns as an excuse.

This perplexing decision seemed to fly in the face of the reason for their trip, namely to win friends, influence people and generally increase positive predisposition towards it as the world's number one football brand. United's snooty and elitist attitude provoked the highly emotional Brazilians, who began to disparage 'The Reds' and their unfriendly stance.

Foul and offensive

Then, following an early tournament game, United boss Sir Alex Ferguson enraged fellow teams by suggesting that play-acting by his team's Mexican opponents was the reason behind the ref's decision to send David Beckham off. This ignored the fact that Beckham had clearly committed a serious foul on the field of play.

Team tactics

When the Super Red's PR machine eventually got itself warmed up, its attempts at promotion were altogether inappropriate given Brazil's status as one of the poorest countries in Latin America and Rio's reputation for widespread homelessness and social hardship. Pictures of Man U's highly paid stars gallivanting on the beach and around the ritzy hotel pool did little to illustrate how much the soccer idols' visit meant to the people for whom football is a religion and a way of life. It patently hadn't occurred to the club that pictures of the players giving away Man U merchandise and soccer balls to kids living in the city's sprawling slums might have been much more appropriate.

LESSONS LEARNT

For a corporation as prominent as Man U to fail to spot and capitalize on the PR potential that this trip offered, was baffling. To bolster its position as football's best-known brand, the club has a reputation to live up to and an identity to project. Plainly, the club was not properly psyched up for the responsibility that such an ambassadorial trip entails. So, this away-from-home result was a lot less flattering than it could have been, if they had really understood the role and value of community relations. As a global sports brand with an international player pool, which profits from helping global sponsors' names to come alive, Manchester United's community extends beyond the UK.

It has as much a responsibility to the football-mad Brazilians as it does to the people in the streets surrounding its home ground in England's North West. A bad reputation – accrued through mismanaged PR – doesn't need a passport to travel; media reportage sees to that.

Stakeholder relations – Airline grounded over PR response

Media spin:
'Passenger taken off flight for drunk pilot joke'
Reuters

Passenger airline America West flew from one PR disaster into another when it overreacted to a customer comment following an incident where two of its pilots were fired for being drunk at the half-wheel.

As if the initial negative publicity over its inebriated employees wasn't bad enough, America West compounded the situation when some of its staff subsequently prevented a woman from flying with them when she jokingly quipped, 'Have you checked your crew for sobriety?' after boarding a flight in San Francisco.

America West's failure to show any sense of humour, far less just take it on the chin, breached a cardinal rule of Public Relations, namely, 'Don't do anything that exacerbates or prolongs the negative situation.' The airline's churlishness again backfired when news of how they'd treated a paying customer spread among its other stakeholders including, of course, the media. The airline's overreaction led to several re-runs of the ejected passenger tale, plus detailed reporting of its prequel.

LESSONS LEARNT

Although widely publicized in the media, this incident also under-lines the importance of internal communications. In the wake of the original incident involving the inebriated pilots, the airline should have prepared and circulated incident briefing notes to its staff, especially those with public-facing duties. This communiqué should have documented the real facts of the case and included advice on what to do in the event of follow-on interest from the media, passengers or the general public. Clear and informative internal communications might just have given America West staff the skills and confidence to handle any flak flying around as a result of the incident. Sometimes, good stakeholder relations don't need to be rocket science, just common sense.

Stunts – Tearing strips off publicity attempt

Media spin:

'Jackson flash a new low'

CBS News

Many people – journalists included – mistakenly believe that creative stunts are to PR activity what they are to circuses: the work of clowns. Of course, because publicity stunts are often the most visible part of PR strategy, the terms 'publicity' and 'PR' have acquired a confused synonymity.

One of the key components in creating a PR stunt is the element of surprise; it might include the strange juxtaposition of a high-profile media star and a giant-sized prop, or the public unveiling of a familiar object presented in an unfamiliar guise. Whatever the choice, the element of theatrical surprise has to be present for the media to be impressed enough to take notice.

But any time a publicity stunt goes awry – such as when pop star Justin Timberlake ripped off a portion of Janet Jackson's costume in a live national broadcast, revealing part of her naked breast – it's conveniently dubbed a PR disaster.

Half-baked at half-time

Timberlake and Jackson are two music stars whose careers depend on widespread media exposure. The former has tried to replace his teen heart-throb image with one that's more raunchy. Janet was simply born into the continual exposure that accompanies being a member of the Jackson family.

Both artistes conspired to develop a publicity stunt that was intended to captivate the attention of the almost 90 million viewers who had tuned in to watch the highlight of the American sporting calendar. Booked to provide the half-time entertainment at the most watched and eagerly anticipated sports event in the United States – the Super Bowl American Football Final – the two danced provocatively, before Timberlake yanked at Jackson's black leather bustier, revealing a breast only partly covered by a metal nipple shield. In sync with his yank, Timberlake smouldered the words, 'I'm gonna have you naked by the end of this song.'

Mixed messages

The stunt, plus Timberlake's perfectly-timed ad-lib, seemed consistent with pre-event publicity promises on the MTV website, which hinted that the performance would feature 'shocking moments' that would ensure that the game 'goes down in history'. MTV – the edgy, teen-oriented satellite music TV channel – had been awarded the contract to supply the Super Bowl's musical entertainment. The stunt wasn't the only thing going down, because Justin and Janet's reputations were pursuing a similar trajectory.

Even non-cynics would have suspected that the revelatory rip was intended to shock, though the shock was equally Timberlake's and Jackson's, as they'd miscalculated the reactions that followed. Broadcaster CBS's switchboard was jammed with protest calls and the Federal Communications Commission received more than 200,000 complaints, prompting its head honcho to comment that the unveiling was 'a classless, crass, deplorable stunt' before launching a high-profile probe into the incident.

With the Bush administration voicing its concerns amid the announcement of a media-wide crackdown on sexually explicit material being broadcast on TV and radio, the stunt was elevated to the level of a national scandal, and quickly dubbed 'Nipplegate' by the media.

A sorry affair

The fact that the two music stars were unprepared for the backlash showed in the conflicting excuses each offered for the disrobing: wannabe bad boy Justin kept on apologizing for any offence caused. After all, the 'PR stunt' was threatening several of his lucrative sponsorship deals. For her part, Janet – initially through a spokesperson – apologized yet conceded the stunt was intentional, though not meant to go as far as it did. Her bra was supposed to be exposed, not her breast, she insisted.

Against a cacophonic background, which had everyone apologizing to everyone else, the National Football League distanced itself from MTV, which had produced the segment, by saying they were unlikely to get the job again. In turn, MTV distanced itself from the artistes by saying it had been 'punked' by them. Although pleading ignorance to any of what had gone on, CBS nonetheless felt compelled to apologize to its audiences. It was crisis management gone mad, with everyone expressing 'concern' while trying to deflect blame onto various third parties.

Eventually, Timberlake and Jackson sang off the same song sheet, saying the boob 'boob' was due to a 'wardrobe malfunction'. But then the costume creators kicked up a public stink at the inference that its clothing was sub-standard; after all, they, too, had a reputation to protect.

It was all too much for one Tennessee woman, who launched a widely publicized, multi-million dollar damages lawsuit against the prank's protagonists after being 'traumatized' by the exposé.

Flak flew the world over, with newspapers debating the incident and audiences clamouring to replay it. This made the malfunction the most searched-for clip in Internet history. Janet Jackson's profile was the highest it had been in almost a decade, which should have been good news for the timely release of her new CD, 'Damita Jo'. But her reputation, like her brassiere, was temporarily in tatters. She was 'dis-invited' from the Grammys in the week after 'Nipplegate' and her single, which should have been boosted by all the advance publicity, received a tepid retail reception.

LESSONS LEARNT

Publicity stunts are designed to grab the attention of a largely cynical and often passive media, who demand to be impressed or entertained by publicists or press agents. Those who create these stunts, however, run the risk and accept the fact that they're going to lose some control over how the stunt will be reported; that depends heavily on the media's interpretation of the event.

Publicity stunts also aim to get the attention of a widespread audience. However, herein lies the fundamental flaw of Janet and Justin's stunt: they totally misjudged their audience and, along with it, the fluid morality of the US public. Although both stars were favourites on MTV and were performing while notionally in MTV's employ, the Super Bowl's TV audience has a very different demographic and, hence, very different sensibilities than an MTV audience. With mums and dads, kids, aunts, uncles plus grandmas and grandpas gathered around TV sets, the Super Bowl may be the United States' biggest viewing audience, but it's traditionally its most mainstream and conservative.

Colossal viewer numbers are irrelevant if all you are going to do is offend the masses and make them turn against you and your commercial partners.

Ascribing to proven issues management principles, Janet and Justin apologized using written statements. They appeared on opinion-forming TV and radio shows to personally express contrition and concern. Janet even released a Video News Release reiterating regret, but the weight of negative coverage far outstripped any positives that the audience could have taken out of the incident.

The stars' repeated bleating and apologizing merely portrayed them as being as lame as the ill-conceived stunt was in the first place.

Targeting, Television, Testimonials

Targeting – Scouting for revenue

Media spin:

'Birds sing – but campers can't unless they pay up'

Star Tribune

The American Society of Composers, Authors and Publishers (ASCAP) is a non-profit organization representing songwriters and composers. Basically, ASCAP's job is to police the use of written music and ensure that licence fees – which grant permissions to use registered songs and jingles – are collected and redistributed to its members.

ASCAP continually needs to elevate its own profile so that it's able to highlight the obligations of organizations that use music that is copyright protected. In one communications campaign, ASCAP produced a direct mail piece informing the USA's 8,000-plus summer camps that federal copyright law required them to pay fees to ASCAP for any songs they broadcast during camp times.

No smoke without campfire

It appeared that ASCAP wanted – for the first time in its history – to collect fees every time a party of boy scouts or girl guides sang songs around a campfire. At the same time as the mailer's release, ASCAP CEO John Lo Frumento was reported in the *Wall Street Journal* as saying that just as summer camps buy paper, twine and glue for crafts, they needed to pay for using music, too. Adding insult to injury, he also signalled a willingness to sue those summer camp operators and, by inference, the cherubic scouts and guides who didn't pay their song licence rights. It all sounded so unbelievable, which is what made it absolutely perfect for news copy.

Chorus of disapproval

Subsequent to the *Wall Street Journal* story, a rash of editorials across the USA lampooned ASCAP for its killjoy attempts to make a buck out of one of childhood's simplest pleasures: singing campfire songs. The negative publicity created not so much ripples but waves of protest from both the public and also ASCAP's own members. Rearguard efforts by ASCAP spokespeople to douse the flames had little effect on the voluble protests against its plans to levy the summer camps. Responding to the negative criticism, ASCAP sang out a set of classics including, 'never sought nor was it ever its intention to', 'encourage the use of music everywhere', as well as the evergreen 'quoted out of context'. You know how those songs go...

The same old song

The problem was allowed to brew as, subsequent to the protests, ASCAP CEO Lo Frumento went to ground, refusing to answer questions or give comment; this effectively represented a dereliction of PR duty by the CEO, particularly when the words causing the brouhaha were of his choosing.

Between the lines

Behind the sensationalist reporting, the truth was almost exclusively overlooked. ASCAP was actually only interested in pursuing those larger summer camps that staged rock or pop concerts and larger-scale parties where music is broadcast via public address systems. It wasn't chasing boy scouts and girl guides for nickels and dimes. However, it had purchased a master mailing list of all 8,000 camps and indiscriminately block-mailed them all, thereby causing alarm and disquiet among the smaller camps. Each of these camps was only too happy to give interviews to interested media.

Combine the camps' alarm with the media's 'money-grabbing' soundbites and there was enough tinder to keep the campfires burning for many a night. It was a fatigued ASCAP VP, Vincent Candilora, who eventually conceded, 'What can I say? We bought a mailing list. We should have done more research.'

LESSONS LEARNT

Many organizations seem inclined to skip over the need to pre-research communications campaigns, viewing it as an unnecessary cost burden. Yet what was the cost in terms of reputation damage? Simply taking the time to sift a database and tailor the right message to the right audience would have done much to minimize this nightmare for ASCAP.

And then there was the puzzling decision by ASCAP's main man to go mute when faced with media enquiries. The concept of 'no comment' is a clichéd anachronism in today's soundbite-savvy business world. As CEO, Lo Frumento should have been ready to account for the words and deeds of the entity he represented, and to counter the impact the incident was having on his organization. As seen time and time again, the simple but sterling rule for handling media relations was broken: if you don't want something quoted, don't say it.

Television – Bogged down

Media spin:

'That sinking feeling when PR goes pear-shaped'

The Scotsman

Vauxhall Motors – the UK arm of carmaker General Motors – had invested millions of pounds to improve and restyle its Frontera Sport all-terrain vehicle (ATV), which had been losing ground in the 'soft adventurer' section of the automotive market.

Having upgraded all its Frontera models, new preview vehicles were made available to journalists and TV programme-makers. The aim was to secure significant national media coverage demonstrating that the recent modifications had rendered the Frontera a better, more robust and more capable 4x4 vehicle.

Wheel spin

A relatively new and slightly maverick TV show called 'Driven' was given one of the ATVs for review. The filming location chosen by its team of enthusiastic correspondents was an English coastal town called Weston-super-Mare. In taking the new Frontera onto the sandy, coastal terrain, *Driven* proceeded to sink £20,000 worth of state-of-the-art motoring technology in 20 ft of gritty sludge. In truth, any ATV or SUV vehicle would have struggled to fare any better in such aggressively adverse conditions.

Having already seen the new pride of its 4x4 fleet scuppered, Vauxhall felt justifiably aggrieved by the decision by *Driven* to screen the whole sorry, soggy scenario, thereby sinking the new car's reputation even before it had the chance to properly debut in showrooms. Not only that, but the programme-makers ran snippets of the footage as trailers for the programme, in order to attract and boost audience figures. A perversely enthusiastic public tuned in to watch the Frontera's misfortune and both pre- and post-screening, other media preyed upon the incident.

Driven to distraction

Any organization that provides access to its products or services to have them reviewed by the media, needs to accept that they're relinquishing control and that there's always the possibility that something untoward could happen. It could be argued that Vauxhall could have been more rigorous in policing the use of its Frontera (especially with a team of young guns). Then again, the Frontera was supposed to be an adventure vehicle capable of going virtually anywhere, accessible beaches included. You might also wonder if Vauxhall was 'stitched up' by *Driven*, which, as a fledgling TV show, needed to boost viewing figures for its own survival? As I suggested, few vehicles would have been able to weather the boggy quicksands, so where were the journalistic ethics in screening a segment they knew would cause irreparable damage to the vehicle's – and the Vauxhall marque's – image?

LESSONS LEARNT

To calculate the damage to the reputation of a 4×4 promoted to motorists as a vehicle 'that positively attracts those looking for adventure in their lives' was nigh impossible. To guess at the irreparable breach of trust between Vauxhall and the 'Driven' team is probably a whole lot easier. The relationship between PR practitioners and the media is not an equitable one; the media has its very own agenda and, more than that, it usually resents what it sees as the PR's only agenda – free publicity. This inherent suspicion means that PR people need to be aware of the unpredictability and volatility of the relationship that exists when dealing with the media.

Apparently, Vauxhall tried to appeal to *Driven's* more reasonable side but, having exhausted all attempts to get the programme-makers to be 'fair' about the incident, it couldn't take any action that might have created greater enmity between itself, rest of its range – and 'Driven' and possibly other media titles. As is often the case, it seems that the media possesses a distinctly cannibalistic taste for biting the PR hand that often feeds it.

Testimonials – Word is out

Media spin:
'Microsoft "regrets" Mac-to-PC ad'
www.cnetnews.com

Glowing praise from satisfied customers is a form of ammunition favoured by many PR practitioners. Like 'word of mouth' advertising, testimonials have an air of authenticity and credibility. Given the current proliferation of online e-pinion groups, user testimonials can be more immediate and potent than editorial generated by other media.

Shift

Microsoft found itself drawn into PR controversy when a testimonial from a delighted user, who had apparently shifted her preference from Macintosh to Windows XP hardware, was posted on the Microsoft website. Unfortunately, the fulsome praise was all too easily shown to have originated from a PR consultant at one of the firms working on the Microsoft promotion.

By tracing source code – electronic clues on the posting – which revealed both the author's name and the software licence holder, internet sleuth Slashdot was able simultaneously to show that the testimonial was a fake. This 'unveiling' also revealed that the PR people working on this technology account were nowhere near as technologically savvy as they should have been.

Delete word

Responsively, Microsoft removed the article almost as quickly as word was spreading that the falsification had been rumbled, though not before news of the deceit had been extensively posted and forwarded by internet-watchers. Extensively flamed on online forums for the 'lie', Microsoft's reputation had been sullied.

LESSONS LEARNT

When testimonials are shown to be the handiwork of PR consultants, it undermines the validity of the concept of independent endorsement and the integrity of PR representatives everywhere. But as long as there are no punitive penalties for telling lies or breaching codes of ethical behaviour, and as long as there are financial returns to be made on both the client and PR consultancy side, this probably won't be the last incident where testimonials are 'created' to sway a target audience.

For those readers who are still intent on adding the occasional 'testimonial' to a client website, you must apparently remember to click 'File', then 'Properties' to cover up the all too revealing 'e-traces'. But before you rush to do so, consider this: why would anyone posting a genuine testimonial go to all the trouble of making themselves anonymous?

Undercover Operations

Undercover operations – A royal pardon

Media spin:
'A wolf in sheik's clothing'
www.time.com

PR has infiltrated every stratum of society. Even the UK's Royal Family, at one time above having to court public opinion, has had to deploy PR to rebuild its reputation following a number of years of bad press.

So, when Prince Edward married London PR executive Sophie Rhys-Jones, who became Sophie, Countess of Wessex, the royals might have thought that their PR nightmares were at an end. Unfortunately, they were only just beginning.

Sheik-rattled and rolled

There had been previous controversy over claims that Prince Edward had tried to leverage his royal connections to develop business for his TV production company, Ardent Films. Now, fresh evidence emerged that suggested that his new bride was cast from exactly the same mould.

Some mischief-making – or just editorial-making – by the tabloid *News Of The World* lured Sophie into a fictitious new business scenario with a supposed Arab sheik. The fake sheik – in reality a *NOTW* journalist – taped how Sophie seemed all too willing to use her royal connections to develop new business and publicize her existing clients. In the newspaper sting, Sophie discussed private and delicate family matters seemingly with a view to winning a lucrative – but imaginary – new PR account.

She talked about her husband's struggling production company, Ardent, and of its many royal business and connections. She also talked of the couple's financial status, including their inability to meet the running costs of their royal mansion in Surrey. Her candid revelations, perhaps designed to bring the 'sheik' into her confidence, hinted that Sophie was bringing new meaning to the phrase 'PR transparency'.

All the while, it was conveniently forgotten that the 'sting' had been engineered by a tabloid paper, hell-bent on selling more newsprint.

Regaling her story

When the sham was revealed to Sophie and her fellow PR company directors, this matter of high public interest catalysed the involvement of yet another communications specialist who also failed to cover himself in glory. The Queen's director of communications, Simon Walker, made the brave judgement call of offering the *News of the World* a new, formal interview with Sophie in attempts to secure a more sympathetic portrayal of the royal couple.

This second interview gave Sophie a chance to redress her earlier indiscretions but, amazingly, Sophie candidly revealed even more details about her royal role, then discussed her husband's much debated sexuality and even her own fertility. The subsequent headline in the *NOTW* exclusive – 'My Edward's Not Gay' – actually perpetuated the rumours over Edward's sexuality, despite Sophie's clumsy attempts to quell them.

LESSONS LEARNT

What allegedly experienced PR person reveals details of her very public private life to a potential new client in a formative meeting, just to win business?

For a supposedly savvy PR – but also a high-profile celebrity – to tell a stranger that she may have to resort to IVF to get pregnant represented an unnecessarily candid admission. After all, the distinction between private and public life does not exist for celebrities, meaning their every move and word is under scrutiny, 24/7. Then, when another seasoned practitioner enters into a media pact with the original entrappers, then passes a controversial interview for publication, we see evidence of near desperation.

Sophie Wessex, the *News of the World*, Prince Edward and Simon Walker; none came out the other end of this operation with reputations intact. And yet again, PR's reputation was dragged through the mud in a case littered with questionable ethics and bewildering decision-making.

Video News Releases, Viral Marketing

Video News Releases – Video killed the media star

Media spin:

'US videos, for TV News, come under scrutiny'

New York Times

While the practice of using press releases to stimulate media interest has remained largely unchanged over the past half century, pitching ideas to TV show and internet content producers is perhaps best done via Video News Releases (VNRs). As TV and the internet are visual media, it makes sense to pitch stories to each in visual terms. The objective of producing a VNR is to create broadcast quality audio-visual footage, which can be used by journalists for background information or, if you're a lucky PR person, future broadcast.

Karen Ryan, a multi-talented US media practitioner, got herself in hot water when it was suggested she was attempting to pass off PR-generated VNR-style material as bona fide news reportage. At the time of the allegations, Ryan was running a PR consultancy offering a variety of services, from crisis management to media relations and, also, the production of VNRs.

Prior to her PR consultancy days, Ryan was a seasoned media pro with more than 20 years' expertise as a producer, reporter and TV news anchor, so she was certainly capable of delivering professional standard voice-overs. So professional, in fact, that one VNR featuring Ryan vocally reporting on the updated benefits of Medicare in the United States, were aired by many TV stations as legitimate news footage.

PR by hooker, by crook

Not that this would necessarily have upset the client, the US government's Department of Health and Human Services. After all, it was getting its message across. Nor would it trouble the PR firm that had engaged a Washington video production company to compile the clip (and hire Karen for the voice-over). Their work was obviously of broadcast standard. Ryan herself would doubtless have been equally flattered that having previously jumped the media fence for a career as a PR counsellor, she still hadn't lost any of her old reporting nous and polish.

But the VNR did upset a phalanx of media led by the *New York Times*. It ran a front-page investigation into the Bush administration's predilection for hiring media shills who could generate favourable publicity for recent amendments to Medicare legislation.

Other media slurs by notable chat show luminaries, including Jay Leno and Jon Stewart, called Karen a hooker, a crook, a phoney, a hired propagandist and an actress, as well as a PR consultant.

By any other name

Feeling her professional reputation under attack, Karen refuted most of these allegations, insisting that she only engaged in 'a standard, acceptable practice, namely, narrating a VNR'. But more aggressively, she called the media's professionalism into question for, a) not asking for or reporting her version of the story, and b) for not properly identifying the VNR story's source to its audiences.

Of course, this latter claim cuts across the fact that many VNRs – Ryan's Medicare one included – feature a 'reporter' who narrates the thread of the story, notionally as part of the pitch. Then again, perhaps there's a secret hope that the VNR material supplied might be used in its entirety? For genuine authenticity – and Ryan herself corroborated this on her website – some PR narrators even sign off by stating their location, name and what they were doing there, like, 'In Washington, I'm Karen Ryan reporting.' And that single line was where the line between spin and news became blurred in this incident. Of course, it would have sounded absurd were Ryan to have signed off, 'In Washington, I'm Karen Ryan, PR Consultant-cum-voice-over artist, laying down a guide narration.'

The channels that broadcast the VNR were not without blame in this case. They put one over on their audience by letting them believe that Ryan was a genuine – their genuine – reporter.

LESSONS LEARNT

The Medicare case saw all VNRs denounced as evil and insidious, but that's patently not the case. VNRs can enable cash-starved not-for-profit organizations to get important information to key audiences and can be invaluable for disseminating information when issues affecting national health or product recalls arise.

Similarly, some resource-poor media newsrooms grudgingly appreciate that VNRs help them to transmit news stories accompanied by professionally shot footage, which they otherwise couldn't have accessed but which their audience appreciates.

Ryan may have been unaware of a longstanding guideline for VNR good practice, suggested by the Public Relations Service Council, which states that 'persons interviewed in the VNR must be accurately identified by name, title and affiliation on the video'. *Affiliation* is the key word.

But as Ryan insists that the VNRs were clearly labelled with the client name and the VNR's source, it throws the spotlight back onto the media who lazily adopted the footage. If Ryan's insistence on the 'labelling' point is true, then the professionalism of some of the United States' leading titles – that claimed that the VNRs were not identified as coming from government sources – is worthy of equal scrutiny and reproach.

The case also raises the interesting question of conflict of interest. The PR consultant always has the opportunity to decline an offer of work if he or she feels that handling the contract could create an ethical dilemma. Of course, with so many consultants jumping media fences, eschewing membership of professional organizations and multi-tasking communications outputs to turn a buck, the potential for conflicts of interest is perhaps greater than ever before.

Although Public Relations is a multi-faceted discipline, many of the consultants working in the field are still only hired because of their ability to guarantee that their clients get exposure in news media. And the reality is that despite this furore, there's still a definite market for good VNR materials. With compelling news angles, interesting and sharp interviews, professionally shot footage all delivered in a contemporary broadcast news format, you stand a good chance of getting 'on air'.

At best, this was a genuinely relevant piece of news information that media outlets were free to interpret and edit as they saw fit. At worst, it was a knowing and slick attempt to hoodwink the media and its audiences.

Viral marketing – Maize of deception

Media spin:

'Companies are creating false citizens to change the way we think'

The Guardian

One of the biggest gripes about PR is the seemingly invisible way that it manages to exert its influence, leaving the more inquisitive of us wondering if – or after the event, how – we were so easily duped.

For the most part, PR consultants prefer that the mechanics – though not the results – of their work go unnoticed. The less evidence there is of PR participation, then the greater the chance that the information presented will be taken at face value. Awareness of PR involvement usually only serves to put people on alert that something Machiavellian is afoot.

So, when attempts by an online lobbying company to covertly influence opinion on behalf of its client Monsanto were uncovered by journalist Andy Rowell and an eco-campaigner called Jonathan Matthews, there were red faces all round as the PR cover was blown.

Tasteless

Food grower/engineer Monsanto has not been flavour of the month since it became embroiled in controversy over its plans to encourage people to eat the kinds of genetically modified foods it produces. But when it was linked to attempts to ridicule and discredit two researchers who claimed that genetically modified pollens actually helped to rot crops, it left a bitter taste for anyone who heard the Monsanto name.

When the two University of California researchers produced a paper claiming GM pollen had damaged vast swathes of Mexican maize, one was quickly offered a lucrative research job if he held back from publishing his work. When he declined, the same person who had made the employment offer allegedly threatened to harm the researcher's kids.

Nature's way

Soon after, the research – unflattering to biotech companies and harmful to their attempts to liberalize legislation pertaining to GM foods – was published by *Nature* magazine. Straight away, e-mails began to appear on an online scientific forum, questioning the motives and integrity of the two researchers and the academic rigour of their published study. A flood of others quickly followed these e-mails, all seeming to share the views of the initial ones that attacked the research published by *Nature*. In fact, the criticism escalated to such a volume that the magazine's editor decided to print what amounted to an editorial apology for publishing the article.

A diet of misinformation

A pluralist society should welcome debate and the exchange of different opinions, yet those who looked into the source of these e-mails were dismayed and angered by what they found. And not for the first time, those cast in the worst light were the PR people.

Rowell and Matthews found that the original e-mails attacking the 'maize' researchers came from Mary Murphy and Andura Smetacek, both of whom were traced back through e-mail code clues as having links to Bivings, Monsanto's online communications advisers.

Murphy was directly traced to her hotmail address, yet denied being in the employ of industry players and castigated her inquisitors for having made up their minds about biotech. The strange thing was, though, neither Rowell nor Matthews had even mentioned biotech to Murphy in the course of their conversation. 'Smetacek' was eventually linked to a website registered to and emanating from the Bivings group.

Similarly, the website where the original flak against the paper was posted was run by a Professor Prakash whose e-mails, again, showed linkage to the main server hosted by Bivings. Cosy, but probably not completely impartial, you might suspect.

LESSONS LEARNT

Where the stakes are high and the management – or manipulation – of public opinion is of paramount importance, PR tactics can seemingly morph into industrial espionage and PR practitioners into sabotage agents adopting any tactics needed to derail positions that counter the one(s) desired by their clients.

So the calls for greater PR transparency will continue, probably in parallel with the efforts by some PR practitioners to ensure that their identities remain hidden as they battle to influence the minds of target audiences. Thanks to some underhand and undercover manoeuvres, the quest for hearts may be harder than ever for PR to win.

Once again, we find an incident of compromised ethics, the only real question is whose: the PR consultants or the clients who pay them?

This case is extensively documented by journalist and author George Monbiot on www.monbiot.com, to whom thanks is due for his cooperation.

World Wide Web

World Wide Web 1 – Kick in the teeth

An e-mail campaign initiated by UK menswear retailer Burtons around the time of the Euro 2000 football championships in France, illustrated how the rush to capitalize on a promotional opportunity totally overlooked any potentially negative PR fallout.

The e-mail, featuring a celebratory boast that England had made it to the tournament's quarter finals, was sent to a non-geographically defined database in Britain, along with suggestions that patriotic fans should buy England branded merchandise from Burtons' online store, without delay.

Of course, when England-headquartered Burtons claimed that 'we've done it', it was only referring to the England team's progress in the tournament.

Digital signal

So, when this digital communiqué was received by hitherto placid Burtons' customers in Scotland, the response was reciprocally digital and of the two-fingered variety. Scotland – England's arch enemy in football and many other fields besides – hadn't even qualified to participate in the tournament, far less reach the quarter finals. So to be invited to participate in the gloating that accompanied England's progress only added insult to Scottish soccer injury.

Showing a complete lack of appreciation for Celtic sensitivities, Burtons' offending e-mail ended with the following epitaph: 'And for those plucky but proud losers, we've still got some Ireland products.'

Scots online circulated the e-mail condemning what they saw as yet another example of English sporting arrogance. Many expressed their dissatisfaction by voting with the organ that's dearest to their Caledonian hearts – their sporran. If Burtons had been looking for a way to undermine the goodwill and brand affinity earned by its online store north of Hadrian's Wall, it had found it. The company's slightly exuberant commercial jingoism put a bit of a dent in the retailer's Scottish turnover.

LESSONS LEARNT

In the modern communications landscape, with its manifold abilities to narrowcast messages, there's very little excuse for companies to say the wrong thing to the wrong people. Good online databases should contain enough data for the sender to know that the communiqué will be well received at its destination. But this involves taking the time to carefully tailor the message. More than this, there is always room for PR consultation to help evaluate whether any form of media communication has potentially negative ramifications.

In Burtons' case, it appeared that the desire to engage in a low-cost, mass-reach communications campaign managed to override any thought of targeting the message, thereby damaging the company's hitherto good name in Scotland.

World Wide Web 2 – Room for improvement

Media spin:
'Online complaint about hotel service scores'
USA Today

The extent to which the grapevine-like power of the internet has challenged the historical potency of 'word-of-mouth' communication was never more clearly illustrated than in the case of Hilton Hotels' Doubletree Club in Houston, USA. Following an exchange between a hotel reservations clerk and would-be guests, the web's influence on corporate reputation was manifestly demonstrated, as was the ability of one employee to have a cataclysmic bearing on corporate reputation.

This tale started when two Seattle-based internet consultants, Tom Farmer and Shane Atchison, tried to book into the Doubletree where they had made 'guaranteed reservations'.

Hostile reception

Although they had arrived for check-in at the pretty unorthodox time of 2 am, they felt secure, knowing that their beds were guaranteed. Or so they thought. But at check-in, they were quickly disabused of that notion by a night clerk who curtly informed them that the hotel was now full and that they would have to find accommodation elsewhere. Not only had these guests made a guaranteed reservation with the hotel, the manner in which the clerk treated them defied description, although sneering and obnoxious came pretty close. At one point in their conversation, the clerk even rebuked the pair who, after a long day, just wanted to relax in their rightful room.

PowerPoint of view

Smarting, the two web consultants went away and set about creating a scathing but entertaining PowerPoint presentation. Entitled 'Yours A Very Bad Hotel', it documented the entire incident, including some of the unbelievable exchanges with the clerk. They then e-mailed the presentation to the hotel's management and copied it to a few friends and associates who they thought might like to hear of their bad experience.

The presentation quickly became one of the most sought-after viral e-mails ever produced. It was quickly forwarded to e-mail inboxes all over the world, from Houston to Hanoi and everywhere in between. Hard copies of the PowerPoint were printed off, photocopied and distributed among the travelling sales community throughout the United States. Not surprisingly, the Doubletree Club quickly became the hospitality industry's biggest joke and a stay-away destination for commercial travellers and holiday-makers alike. Traditional media commentators, too, picked up on the news and published damning editorials, which discussed corporate indifference and the power of the Web as an influencer of public opinion.

Subsequently, Farmer and Atchison personally received over 3,000 e-mails, most of them supportive. The hotel's management responded quickly and with equal amounts of magnanimity and good grace. Doubletree apologized unreservedly and showed its contrition by offering to donate $1,000 to a charity nominated by Farmer and Atchison. It also vowed to revisit its employee-training programme to ensure that the likelihood of such an incident ever occurring again was greatly minimized if not made completely impossible. Additionally, one of Doubletree's senior vice presidents agreed to participate in a live Netcast discussion with Farmer and Atchison demonstrating that the hotel chain took the issue very seriously.

LESSONS LEARNT

The key lesson from this episode is that brand image rests on the moment-to-moment experiences of every customer who interacts with that brand. For Doubletree, the experience of two guests caused a geographically widespread crisis of confidence in its service offering. But it's equally true that corporate reputation can be influenced by the company's response to a crisis. As Hilton management demonstrated, it's important that dialogue is not lost but is maintained long enough to ensure that any damage to perceptions of the brand can be repaired.

The Doubletree Club may have been powerless to prevent the PR disaster caused by a surly member of its staff, but its subsequent apologies, expression of genuine regret, willingness to 'face the music' and the remedial action of revising staff training did ensure that the brand was seen to be doing the right thing to repair confidence, and doing it immediately after the initial gaffe had been perpetrated.

XXXX Factor

XXXX Factor – Fail is a four-letter word

The advent of a revolutionary tilting mechanism that allowed British Rail's new Advanced Passenger Train (APT) to corner more efficiently and travel at top speeds of around 155 mph – shaving valuable minutes and even hours off rail journey times – seemed certain to engineer colossal PR coverage.

Exhaustively tested over a 13-year period which eventually saw the APT transfer from the drawing board to the track, the train's media launch in 1981 was possibly the most eagerly anticipated – and PR-hyped – event of the year.

But on its maiden voyage from Glasgow Central to London Euston – and in the presence of many of the UK's leading transport correspondents – the ground-breaking APT inexplicably decided that it was not quite ready to face a potentially adoring public. Breaking down midway on its public debut, the public outing ended up in public humiliation with the APT being towed back to base.

This led to a torrent of stifled expletives from British Rail management and its communications team as a bemused and ammunition-primed cohort of journos was allocated alternative transport – buses – to get them to their destination.

LESSONS LEARNT

Sometimes, despite all PR's best efforts, it simply can't engineer the coverage that it would like to generate.

Youth Marketing

Youth marketing – Knickers in a twist

Media spin:
'Abercrombie pulls racy catalog from stores'
USA Today

In marketing a new line of children's underwear, Ohio-based apparel retailer Abercrombie & Fitch really got conservative US knickers in a twist.

Selling thong (aka G-string) undies with the motto 'eye candy' to girls as young as 10, it faced allegations from a multiplicity of stakeholder groups that it was fostering paedophilia. Criticism came from several influential publications including The *Wall Street Journal*, *The LA Times* and the *San Francisco Chronicle*, as well as concerned Christian and parent groups. Affiliates of the American Family Association inundated Abercrombie & Fitch stores and offices with thousands of e-mails and protest phone calls. This encouraged similar groups like the American Decency Association to call on all of its members to boycott the 110-year-old retailer's merchandise.

Abercrombie & Fitch had little choice but to withdraw the offending panty line but rather than do it with good grace and humility (as best practice issues management models prescribe), it did so muttering under its breath. It said the product line was intended to be lighthearted and cute and that any misreading of this existed only in the eyes of the beholder.

You might have thought all the negative publicity would encourage A&F to exercise a little more restraint in its marketing affairs. After all, it had previously been publicly chided for selling 'Two Wongs Can Make It White' Chinese laundry T-shirts, deemed to be racially offensive to Asian Americans. And before that, the retailer had felt the wrath of Mothers Against Drink Driving (MADD) after publishing potent alcohol recipes in its clothing catalogue, targeted at kids under the legal driving age. But it was belligerently bullish.

So, the firm's promotional 'magalog' continued to draw wrath from a fresh crop of stakeholders including women's organizations, politicians, media pundits and even the State of Illinois. The latter slated the company – now dubbed Abercrombie & Crotch – for its 300-page 'soft porn' catalogue, which had variously promoted the joys of threesomes, oral sex and group masturbation.

Bottom line

Abercrombie & Fitch's 'shockvertising' catalogue, featuring teenage nudity, foul language and sex advice, resulted in the company receiving more than 300 calls an hour as a store boycott gained momentum. One result of this, however, was that it made the 'magalog' totally infamous and a highly prized item that fetched $120 at an online auction. 'Good' bad publicity, as it were.

The overwhelmingly negative press coverage over the pre-teen G-strings and explicit magalog was hurting the company's 600-plus stores and its bottom line. In-store sales slumped and its stock market value followed suit. The latter was doubtless aided by the decision by action group Citizens for Community Values to take out an ad in the *Wall Street Journal*. Aimed at investors' conservative sensibilities, it challenged them on their decision to do business with the A&F smut-mongers.

So, with the National Coalition for the Protection of Children and Families also e-mailing its membership instructions on how they could run their own anti-Abercrombie campaigns, the Ohio retailer withdrew its magalog from the shelves. Again, with little thought on how to appropriately handle the PR dynamics of the incident, the retailer did so with a defiant barb at its detractors, saying the magalog was only temporarily making way for new product lines and that its editorial policy would remain unchanged in future.

LESSONS LEARNT

Like a great yarn, this case study had everything: sex, controversy, money and a notional battle between the forces of good and evil. The only thing lacking, it seemed, was any kind of role for Public Relations, which could have facilitated dialogue between the protagonists.

With a carefully considered strategy, A&F might have managed to retain its edgy proposition for its younger consumers without alienating its more conservative business stakeholders. It can be done, although it entails a bit of application to first segment your audience, then communicating the messages that best support your relationship with each segmented group. If A&F wanted to really get into the teen psyche, it could even have said sorry for its indiscretions, then continued doing more of the same. After all, that's what we all do when we're teenagers.

To outsiders, it looked like Abercrombie & Fitch was suffering most, with sales at stores seriously affected and a historically solid reputation sullied. Its PR response was failing to support the dialogue that it needed to have with all its key stakeholders. It takes a lot of money to create and maintain a brand image, but at a stage when that image fails to support the best interests of the business behind the brand, then it might be said that it's simply too costly to continue supporting.

Zephaniah

Zephaniah, Benjamin – Poetic licence

Media spin:
'Met invitation leaves poet lost for words'
The Guardian

London's Metropolitan Police force was keen to promote the presence and work of its Positive Action Team (PAT), an arm of the law responsible for recruiting and developing police officers from ethnic minority groups.

Attempting to publicly communicate the force's wholehearted commitment to racial integration, the PAT's communications chief, Denise Milani, decided to use part of a poem called 'London Breed'. Written by acclaimed London-based poet Benjamin Zephaniah, it discussed – and at times 'dissed' – the spirit of multiculturalism in the UK capital.

Proceeding at pace with artwork for campaign posters, Denise belatedly asked Zephaniah, the author, for his permission to use his work in the PAT campaign. In the process, she dragged the Met into an uncomfortable PR disaster.

Feeling blue

It was only at this juncture that Denise became aware of Rastafarian Zephaniah's somewhat frosty contempt for London's boys in blue, having been unjustifiably stopped and searched by them on numerous occasions. At the time of the Met's approach, Benjamin was actually suing them over one such incident.

The Met's unwitting approach gave an initially dumbfounded but soon capably expressive Zephaniah a topical excuse to talk to the British media. He expounded on the lack of trust between the police and black Britons who, he explained, are often the brunt of racial discrimination by the police. The communications arm of London's Metropolitan Police had managed to further polarize the force and London's black community at a time when it was looking to affirm its credibility as an ally of people of all races, creeds and colours.

'The London Breed is a real celebration of multicultural Britain but the police do not reflect that,' said Zephaniah. 'We are disappointed to learn this request is likely to be refused, as I felt the London Breed closely reflects the Met's positive attitude to diversity in London,' said Ms Milani.

Needless to say, a new creative tack was required for this well-intentioned – but inadequately researched – campaign.

LESSONS LEARNT

One of the greatest weapons in a PR consultant's armoury is an informed awareness of all those things that might impact on organizational reputation.

Most consultants subscribe to media monitors that can supply real time alerts on emerging issues that can affect business operations. And the proactive consultant always has the option to conduct quick and easy secondary research – the web is an excellent resource – that assists with a general 'horizon scan'. Informal networks either inside or outside the organization can also provide useful intelligence that can help shape the most appropriate communications tactics for any given situation. This can also avoid potentially troublesome incidents, such as the one just outlined. Surely someone at the Met's communications team had heard of London's most vocal black poet's differences with the police?

The PR function should operate like an organizational antenna, picking up signals and messages from a variety of sources and then relaying responsive messages back in the other direction. In an ideal world, that is.

Conclusion – What's Making PR Such a Disaster Area?

As my introduction said, this book wasn't written to beat up the PR profession. Rather, in showing how PR practitioners' efforts and those of their various business associates have yielded less than productive results – catalysing PR disasters of one sort or another – I have tried to suggest ways that practitioners and other communicators can become more professional. I used a fairly rudimentary methodology for crystallizing my final thoughts, too.

Looking back at the 'Lessons Learnt' sections, I noted the main points raised by each case. Grouping these into clusters of related topics, I then set about looking for any themes and patterns that were visible in these groupings.

Two main points repeatedly leapt out during this process: the variable standards of both quality and ethics in contemporary PR practice, and the significant role that the media play in the very concept of 'PR disasters'. Yet these were not the only points of interest that arose as I tried to distil the eclectic and sometimes bizarre case studies assembled.

Source material

As the wide variety of examples in this book illustrates, PR disasters can emanate from an endless array of sources, within or outside any organization.

Although different in source, nature, severity, impact and duration, the incidents are linked not just by their snappy media moniker but, more commonly, by their need for a quick yet considered response that will manage the perceptions forming among those watching the 'disaster' unfold.

What the proliferation of these occurrences means for PR staff – the custodians of reputation, the organizational characteristic most affected by PR disasters – is that its practitioners are always going to be busy. That's the good news. PR's job is to create, maintain and protect an organization's reputation among all those groups with whom the organization has any dealings. Unfortunately, PR doesn't always have the clout to counsel on what the ideal organizational behaviour should be; that's the bad news. Therefore, image management without real management power is an ongoing and sometimes thankless task.

This is because the opinions that influence perception – and hence reputation and image – are not permanently 'fixed', but shift and alter at pace with how the organization's different 'publics' are affected by how they, as groups and individuals, encounter or experience the organization. Every single interaction, every 'minute of truth' – the way a clerk treats a customer or how long it takes to access your online banking facility – affects reputation every bit as much as slick communications campaigns do.

Perhaps if PR were given the reins to counsel on appropriate organizational behaviour at every level, more PR disasters would be avoided.

Hearts and minds

The cases outlined and consequences faced underline that it's a very serious matter, this reputation business. With ever-increasing product homogeneity, many companies achieve differentiation in their marketplace through that intangible, 'brand value'. Brands, of course, are largely built upon the perception of a good reputation.

Increasingly, the value of brand image – especially for high-profile, high-spend corporations like Coca-Cola, McDonald's and Nike – is worth a lot more that the value of the entity's material assets, and is increasingly accounted for in companies' financial statements.

Though you can't really see, feel, taste, touch or smell brand 'image', it can have enormous impact in the public's hearts and minds. And that's where most PR battles are fought – the mind, not the media – with PR trying to capture something completely intangible. Because of this wide-ranging brief, PR in its most strategic form is focused on stakeholders and not just target audiences or market sectors.

Essentially, stakeholders comprise all those people and groups that have or should have some kind of vested interest in an organization's activity, because it may affect them in some way. Consequently, PR has become responsible not just for its own actions and efforts. As the chaperone of reputation, it's also responsible for the behaviour of all the related affiliates, associates, executives, employees and suppliers, whose actions – as the *Talespin* cases suggest – can have a bearing on how a company is perceived.

Of course, the most sobering reality for the PR person to come to grips with is that the action of any one individual from absolutely any field can adversely affect the reputation of the collective. And with some factors forever remaining unmanageable and unpredictable, the reality is that attaining a 100 per cent perfect reputation is impossible. But in the court of public opinion, anything less than perfection is more often derided than excused, and judged as being 'disastrous' rather than deemed unfortunate or unforeseeable.

This brings us to our moot point. What exactly is a PR disaster, anyway?

Playing catch-up with catch-all

While the Institute for Crisis Management comes pretty close with its definition of a PR crisis as 'a significant business disruption that stimulates extensive media coverage', a much broader definition prevails.

If you believe everything you read, watch and hear, a PR disaster is anything that could catalyse embarrassing or negative publicity for any given organization. Examples can range from the apparent ineffectiveness of a high-profile re-branding exercise, to the break-down of attempted reconciliation efforts between politicians representing warring factions in the Middle East. The term 'PR disaster' is even accommodating enough to incorporate marital infidelity, as was the case when salacious SMS messages were sent between a star-struck senorita and a soccer star strutting his stuff in Spain; but it's virtually everything in between these three extremes, to boot. It's little wonder that the PR industry is growing so fast.

The common denominator that actually made all three examples seem disastrous was adverse media coverage. This says as much about the media's role in creating PR disasters, as it reflects any truly disastrous impact on the relationships that these three random examples experienced with any of their stakeholders.

It leads to the supposition that a PR disaster – like a PR crisis – can only become so as a result of media involvement or interpretation: what 'spin' the media choose to give any particular 'tale', in other words. There can be no overlooking or diminishing the media's role in creating PR disasters. While media attention can blow an incident up into a PR disaster, it unwittingly narrows perceptions of PR, portraying the discipline as both inept and solely publicity fixated when, in the majority of cases, it is neither.

In order to understand the media's interest in PR disasters, we have to be able to understand what the media want out of their coverage of any news story. The standard answer is ratings, viewers, readers, surfers or listeners, because these are what are said to help the media justify their value, either to advertisers or to government licence-granters. The media's strategy for getting and keeping audiences is simple: pander to audience tastes. These tastes extend, largely, to stories with negative or threatening angles. Scares sell, attracting the attention of audiences much more strongly than ostensibly 'positive' news stories.

Good news is no news

Once, frustrated by press indifference to information about a client's financially generous and community-minded goodwill initiative, I penned a piece for Australian marketers entitled 'Good News is No

News'. When the same client was rumoured to be mired in a minor scandal, the phone rang hot with journalistic interest.

Either via a preordained selection process or through a journalistic filter – again, a form of 'spin' – the majority of stories that 'make the grade' are of the bad news variety. Adding a sensationalist tone to how that story is relayed merely adds a dramatic treatment that's remarkably effective at capturing and keeping audiences. One embattled and cynical journo confided that there were only ever three stories in the history of journalism: 'tut tut', 'that's weird' and 'poor bastard'. And one of his colleagues vouched that most PR disasters conveniently fall into one or all three of these categories at any time.

Digging a little deeper, we hear tell of the pressures that many journalists are under to protect their own careers and prove their individual worth. Many, for example, fear that their job is only as safe as the next titillating story they pen. Add to this restrictions on time and resources to indulge in thorough journalistic investigations, and we can see how the 'disaster' story has become a soft target. And because most modern disasters affect an entity's or organization's image, subeditors have a field day with the compact phrase 'PR disaster', which succinctly conveys that the incident was damaging, embarrassing, image-denting and significant.

Without media pronouncement that any given incident constitutes a PR disaster, I think the majority of organizations would simply deal with the fact that they had erred, and set about righting the wrong with those stakeholders that were most affected, without ballyhoo, fuss or ado. More companies are becoming switched on to their corporate social responsibilities, and those groups that they deal with are increasingly demanding good behaviour.

It's fair to say, though, that the threat of media attention is a great motivator for responsible corporate behaviour, thereby increasing the likelihood that the proper action – initial and remedial – is undertaken. The other side of this coin, however, is that PR personnel spend the bulk of their 'disaster management' time catering to the media's requirements, as opposed to devoting their energies to working with those stakeholders most affected. This is partly because when it comes to any big PR disasters, any organization's stakeholders, whether in the penthouse or on the pavement, look to the media for the verdict on how the crisis is being handled.

Unfortunately, there will always be some companies, assisted by PR or even legal or technical consultants, that will try to inveigle their way out of the responsibilities that they should honour. Ongoing media scrutiny means that most eventually get caught. But that's as much a matter of managerial ethics as it is of disastrous PR efforts.

Quality control

Speaking of disastrous PR efforts, we also need to consider what deterrents exist to dissuade people from becoming cavalier or crooked in the way they practise PR.

There is no enforceable requirement for PR practitioners to join a membership organization before they can practise, far less adhere to an industry-wide code of ethics. Ultimately, practitioners could be expelled from the discipline's professional ranks, yet adverse publicity aside, can continue to practise. It's thought that as few as 1 in 10 PR practitioners belongs to a representative PR organization.

Some of the cases in this book show that there seems to be confusion among 'credible' consultants as to what kind of PR practices are permissible and which are punishable. Some of the biggest PR conglomerates that boast professional affiliation have for years flouted professional guidelines with impunity and little remorse. Add to this the diverse calibre of candidates working in and defecting to the PR profession, and there's a worrying portent for its future professionalism. As the *Daily Telegraph* journalist, Barbara Amiel, remarked on the pre-eminence of unskilled 'spin doctors', 'If they were doctors, they'd be struck off the register.'

Yet to me, Amiel highlights a real quality control issue that may only get worse, particularly given that PR is again finding itself the 'flavour of the marketing month' and all manner of purported PR people, 'relationship marketers' and 'customer relationship managers' vie for a piece of the PR action.

With the PR industry's inability to effectively regulate practitioners, it's left to other powers – ultimately the law courts but more regularly the media – to make PR people pay for their transgressions. Just as vampires hate daylight, no PR person enjoys being positioned close to the source of a PR disaster. PR practitioners hate being in the bright spotlight of negative media publicity every bit as much as their clients do; it's a classic case of dying by the sword they live by.

Collusion course

This brought me to consider the nature of the relationship between PR practitioners and their clients and bosses. How simpatico are they in terms of professional standards and business ethics, at least judged by the cases featured?

Do clients want their PR advisers to help them gain genuine understanding between the organization and its stakeholders, or would they prefer complete influence over the latter? Several case studies featured in the book hint at collusion between PR practitioners and those they try to serve and protect, when it comes to guidelines on behaviour or tactics pursued.

My own experience tells me that client companies often value PR's ability to operate 'under the radar' in a way that none of the other communications disciplines can. In one particular issues management project I handled for an industrial company, I was mildly feted for my ability to covertly counsel several of my client's most influential stakeholders about their forthcoming media interviews, without the investigative journalist concerned being aware of the presence of any PR representation.

My 'invisibility' was maintained right up until I appeared at the scribe's office to chaperone my client as he gave his interview. The journo had wanted to spring a surprise on the client by filming him for the first time watching footage featuring allegations challenging his product's efficacy; I vetoed this, temporarily phasing the journo, but securing greater control of the issue for my client.

Many PR practitioners are hired by clients for similar types of guile – some might call it sneakiness – and this ability to operate covertly can lead to one of journalism's biggest complaints against PR folk, namely, the lack of transparency with which they conduct their business. In the previous anecdote, transparency seemed a negotiable factor for the journo, my client and me.

The question of ethics, whether client, journalistic or PR, will eventually boil down to one of personal judgement. Just because an individual chooses to transgress needn't mean we damn their profession completely.

Crisis. What crisis?

In the end, the bee in my PR bonnet is that the continued conjoining of the terms 'PR' and 'disaster' may be having a negative impact on the reputation of a profession that is supposed to be, somewhat ironically, expert in the image and impression management business.

As someone who values the profession I've both studied and practised, it's even more depressing that PR lacks credible, charismatic and high-profile champions successfully showing the business and broader communities how PR is, above all, a disciplined, ethical and robust profession. Currently, PR's most prominent role models include Alastair Campbell, Max Clifford, Jack O'Dwyer and Michael Levine; which one is PR's true champion?

If there is a glimmer of hope for PR, it's that the people and the organizations that they represent can eventually recover from PR disasters; the Perriers and the Tylenols of the world are testament to that. But if PR wants to repair its own damaged reputation, it's going to take more than just sending out a 'good news' press release to do it. With the prevailing news agenda, who'd publish it anyway?

Just like any other PR disaster scenario, the central party has to be prepared to walk the talk and all practitioners must be willing to play a part. The representative bodies need to draft a rigorous strategic plan, enforce compliance and empower strong, authoritative yet empathetic leaders to execute a results-oriented strategy. Failing that, open and honest dialogue between the industry and its stakeholders would be a start.

The strategy most likely involves having to express concern and regret when negative incidents have occurred, shunning charlatans and putting distance between the profession and perpetrators of poor PR practice. In taking positive, decisive and visible remedial action to restore confidence among those stakeholders most affected, the industry also needs to be more proactive in selling its positive qualities, not just getting noticed for its negative traits. It's a sad fact that very little of the good work of PR practitioners is ever communicated or truly appreciated outside the profession. Maybe, as Evan Dando once said, it's about time.

In concluding, I'm going to go all 'Zen' on you. The Chinese word for crisis is written with two strokes: one representing danger, the other opportunity. As PR's own reputation is at a critical juncture, maybe there's a chance to grab the initiative now and fast repair any reputational damage.

The job of the PR practitioner is inherently fraught with danger, but if the cases featured show us anything, it is that there's always the opportunity to do better by aspiring to best practice models and higher ethical standards. Maybe that way, the outbreak of PR disasters can be minimized and PR's own reputation can be improved.

Index

Also published by Kogan Page

E-PR: The Essential Guide to public relations on the internet
Matt Haig

Ethics in PR: A practical guide to the best practice
Patricia J Parsons

Everything You Should Know About Public Relations
Anthony Davis

How to Advertise: What works, what doesn't – and why
Ken Roman, Jane Maas & Martin Nisenholz

Beyond Branding: How the new values of transparency and integrity are changing the world of brands
Nicholas Ind

Brand Failures: The truth about the 100 biggest branding mistakes of all time
Matt Haig

Brand Management Checklist: Proven tools and techniques for creating winning brands
Brad van Auken

Brand New Brand Thinking: Brought to life by 11 experts who do
Edited by Merry Basking and Mark Earls

Brand Royalty: How the world's top 100 brands thrive and survive
Matt Haig

BRANDchild: Remarkable insights into the minds of today's global kids and their relationships with brands
Martin Lindstrom

The Essential Brand Book: Over 100 techniques to increase brand value
2nd edition, Iain Ellwood

Living the Brand: How to transform every member of your organization into a brand champion
2nd edition, Nicholas Ind

Media Monoliths: How great brands thrive and survive
Mark Tungate

The above titles are available from all good bookshops. To obtain further information, please contact the publisher at the address below:

Kogan Page Limited
120 Pentonville Road
London N1 9JN
United Kingdom
Tel: +44 (0) 20 7278 0433
Fax: +44 (0) 20 7837 6348
www.kogan-page.co.uk